GOODSPEED'S

HISTORY

I0081134

OF
DICKSON COUNTY,
TENNESSEE

Vertical Limits Publishing Co.
Broken Arrow, OK

Goodspeed's History of Dickson County, Tennessee. -- 1st ed.
ISBN: 13: 978-1-942702-00-9
ISBN: 10: 1942702000

Contents

PART ONE

HISTORY OF

DICKSON COUNTY

DICKSON COUNTY lies within the limits of the western iron district of the State, and belongs to that geological division known as the Highland Rim. On the eastern boundary are two small tracts in creek valleys where the Meniscus limestone appears at the surface, but with these exceptions the outcrops are wholly from the silicious group of the Carboniferous age. The chief stone of the county is the St. Louis limestone, which contains the famous coral *Lithostrotion Canadense.* -The stone is cherty, fossiliferous, often crinoidal, sometimes silicious and argillaceous, and is very valuable. There are three large and beautiful caves in the county which have been explored, and are often visited by pleasure seekers. One is near Cumberland Furnace, and has been explored three miles or more. The entrance to this cave is about ten feet square. Another cave is near Roger's Mill, on Yellow Creek; has an entrance about 20x60 feet, and has been explored about two miles. Bowman Cave on Sulphur Fork of Jones' Creek, and about two and one-half miles west of Charlotte, has an entrance of only about four feet square, but opens immediately into a large room. This cave has been explored not over half a mile, and is a great resort for picnics. The scenery in each cave is very beautiful. Charlotte rests upon the *Lithostrotion* beds.

Next to Hickman County, Dickson and Stewart rank as iron counties. The first iron furnace established in the western country was in this county. This was the Cumberland Furnace, which was erected in February, 1793, by Gen. James Robertson. After operating the furnace for several years Gen. Robertson sold the property to Montgomery Bell. The furnace was abandoned by Mr. Bell in a short time and the present Cumberland Furnace erected about half a mile east. This furnace is situated on Barton's Creek, in the Eighth District, and is the only iron establishment in the county now in operation. It is claimed, and has not been refuted, that all the cannon balls used by Gen. Jackson at the battle of New Orleans, during the war of 1812, were cast by this furnace and shipped to that city in keel-boats. The capacity of this furnace is about twelve tons of pig metal per day. The pig metal is hauled on wagons to Cumberland River, a distance of about eight miles, for shipment. Worley Furnace, which was established several years later, was operated up to the year 1874, and was then closed and has remained so. This furnace was situated on Piney River, in the First District. Furnaces were also established and operated for different lengths of time before 1860, as follows: Carroll Furnace and Bellview Furnace, on Barton's Creek in the Sixth District; Piney Furnace on Piney Creek, in the First District; Laurel Furnace on Jones' Creek, and Jackson Furnace on Beaver Dam, in the Fourth District. Iron forges were erected at the same time and in conjunction with the furnaces, as follows: Turnbull and White Bluff Forges on Turnbull Creek, in the Twelfth District; Valley and Jones'

Creek Forges, on Jones Creek, in the Sixth District; Red House Forge on Jones Creek, and Steam Forge near Cumberland River, in the Eighth District. The ore banks are numerous and very rich, and are to be found in almost any part of the county. Those from which ore has been taken in limited quantities for specimens are as follows: The Ticer Bank, one and a half miles from Charlotte, in the Sixth District; the Puckett Bank, three miles south of Burn's Station, in the Fourth District; the Robertson Bank, six miles west of Charlotte, in the Sixth District, and the Contrary Pond Bank, two miles north of the Nashville, Chattanooga & St. Louis Railway, in the Eleventh District

In 1865 parties commenced boring for petroleum in the Jones Creek Valley. Oil was obtained after reaching the depth of 565 feet, and several hundred barrels were utilized. The use of inferior tools, combined with the inexperience of the parties having the project in hand, rendered the enterprise unprofitable, and it was abandoned. A company has lately been organized at Dickson, known as the "Dickson Coal Oil Company," which has in view the prosecution of the search for oil in paying quantities and qualities in the Jones Creek Valley, and the erection of suitable works. The company is composed as follows: J. R. Bryan, Dr. C. M. Lovell, Henry Smith, W. S. Coleman, J. T. Henslee, N. B. Lipe and Edward Techont, the two latter gentlemen living in Carroll County, Tenn. Natural gas is supposed to exist in paying quantities in the above valley, and negotiations are on foot looking to the early development of this resource of the county.

The J. R. Bryan & Co. Lime Works have two kilns in operation one-half mile south of Burn's Station, and J. C. Donegan & Co. have one kiln in operation at their works, a short distance north of the above works. The former company have about $15,000 invested in their establishments, which consists of two large kilns,

with a combined capacity of 200 barrels of lime per day; a stave
and heading factory, which has a capacity of 200 barrels per day,
also a general store, with a stock of about $3,000. About fifty la-
borers are employed at the works. J. C. Donegan & Co. employ
about twelve laborers and have about $10,000 invested in their
works. The barrels used at their kiln are manufactured by J. R.
Bryan & Co. The major portion of the products of these kilns is
shipped to Nashville in bulk, where it commands an average market price, while the barreled lime is shipped into several adjoining
States. The laborers employed at these works live with their fami-
lies in the little valley, and together they form quite a village.

At Colesburg, in the Fifth District, a sumac-mill is operated,
which grinds several tons of leaves per day. This promises to be an
important industry for Dickson County, as the sumac grows in
abundance on all the waste lands, and, when prepared for market,
brings from $70 to $90 per ton. Kingston Station is 506 feet above
the sea level; Turnbull Creek Bottom, 459 feet; Sullivan Creek,
473 feet; six miles west of Kingston Station, on the railroad, 819
feet; eight miles farther west 862 feet; six miles farther west, 915
feet; and Gordon's Creek, 736 feet above. The prominent creeks
are Yellow, Barton's, Jones', Piney, Johnson, Harpeth, Turnbull,
Gordon's, Sulphur Fork and Town Branch of Jones' and Bear.

The first land entries bear evidence of the presence of white
men in this county as early as 1786. These entries were in the nature of military land grants which were issued by the governors of
North Carolina for services rendered in the Continental war, and
were as follows: John Hogg 640 acres, in 1786; John Johnston
1,500 acres and Oliver Smith 640, in 1791; Hezekiah Barnes 350
acres and Edward Dickson 640 acres, in 1792; John King 457 acres
in 1793; James West 4,800 acres, John Davis 1,280 acres, Benjamin E. Randolph 1,000 acres, and Charles Stewart 1,280 acres, in

1795; Aaron Lambert 274 acres, in 1796; Joseph Kemp 274 acres, Charles Stewart 640 acres, George Ward 274 acres, Sterling Brewer 300 acres and Robert Lanier, 640 acres, in 1797; William Hill 320 acres, in 1807; Jesse S. Ross 200 acres, in 1808; William Tynell 360 acres, in 1809; Thomas Mathis 74 acres, in 1810; Thomas Garay 50 acres, Henry Wert 20 ½ acres, and Spilsley Tribble 820 acres, in 1811. Among those who located on the waters of Barton's Creek during the nineties were Gen. James Robertson, who came from Nashville; John Nesbitt, from South Carolina; Hudson Johnson, from North Carolina; Abraham Caldwell, from Ireland; Richard Napier, from Virginia, and Montgomery Bell from Pennsylvania. Those who settled about the same time on Jones' Creek were Christopher Strong, Reace Borran, William Cox, Molton Dickson, James Martin, James Steel and Eleazer Smith, from North Carolina; Robert Harper, from Ireland; John Larkins and Fiel Farrer, from South Carolina, and Gabe Joslin, from Nashville. Johnson's Creek, same time, George Tubbs, from South Carolina; Charles Teal, from Maryland, and William Ward, from Virginia. Yellow Creek, same time, George Turner and John Adams, from Virginia; John Le Masters, from North Carolina, and Jerry Nesbitt, from South Carolina. Turnbull Creek, Edward Tidwell, John Brown, Samuel Sellers, and Minor Bibb, from South Carolina, and Milton Johnson, William and Thomas Gentry and William Pullen, from Virginia. On Piney River, William Hogins, from Virginia, and Nicholas and Hutson Dudley and Thomas Petty, from North Carolina. Other settlers of that period were Robert Crumpler, who came from North Carolina and settled on Town Branch of Jones' Creek, and Thomas Fannel, who came from Virginia and settled near what is now Charlotte. Richard Warway, George Southerland, Hugh McNeiley, Christopher Robertson, Nathan Crumpler, Daniel and Jacob Leach, Daniel Williams, James Nosworthy, William Fussel, James Walker, John Spencer,

Anthony Vanlier, John Hendrickson, Epps Jackson, Elias Napier, Robert and Hicks Boxter, William Doak, William Russell, Lemuel Harvey, Jesse Craft, William Caldwell, John Hall, James Fentress, John Burton, William Brasier, Redner Adams, Thomas Simpson, Robert Stington, Moses Smith, Cornelius Magraw, William Moore, Samuel Parker, Burgiss Harris and Thomas Mitchell were among the settlers who came to Dickson County between 1800 and 1810.

Two block-houses, or forts, were built for protection. These forts were rude but strong log houses, with doors and windows made of puncheons, calculated to withstand both bullets and arrows, and were situated near Cumberland Furnace and the town of White Bluff. There is only one instance on record where the life of a settler was taken by Indians in the county. In 1809 the Indians went upon a general raid, and much property and not a few lives were destroyed. One band of them crossed Duck River and came into this county, and raided the farm of Col. William Garner, on the creek by that name, and, after killing the Colonel, drove away most of his stock. Several large grave-yards used by the Indians are situated in the county. Until 1800 there were no roads through Dickson County, the nearest approach to one being simply a trail, running from the Cumberland River to the head of Yellow Creek, passing through what is now Charlotte. In about 1810 or 1812 a road was established from Nashville to Charlotte, and from the latter place on to the Southern States.

The first man licensed by the county court to keep a general store was John Holland, who, in 1806, opened a store in the county (the location of which cannot be ascertained), and sold dry-goods, notions, groceries and whisky. The same year Burton Scroggins was granted a license to keep an ordinary. The first corn-mills of which there is any recollection were built along in 1800. Probably the first one was on Jones' Creek, and was built by Arter West. The building was a one-story log structure, about 25x30 feet in dimensions, and was water-power. Similar mills were erected about the same time on Jones Creek by Christopher Strong; on Yellow Creek, by John Adams; on Piney River, by William Edwards; also one near the Hickman County line on Piney River, by James Davis. The mills of the present are as follows: First District, corn and saw-mill, water-power, on Piney River, owned by Ira Dugan; Second District, corn-mill, water-power, on branch of Piney River, owned by Buck Murrell; Third District, corn and flour-mill, water-power, on Parker's Creek, owned by Samuel Spencer; Fifth District (Dickson), steam flour-mill, owned by T. F. McCreary; Sixth District, corn-mill, steam-power, on Sulphur Fork, owned by W. M. Larkins; saw-mill, steam, owned by Heath & Jennings; corn-mill, water-power, on Jones' Creek, owned by William Jordon; Seventh District, corn-mill, steam-power, owned by Jacob Hand; Eighth District, corn and flour-mill, steam-power, owned by E. N. Phipps; Ninth District, corn mill, water-power, and saw-mill, steam-power, owned by Thomas Rogers; Twelfth District (White Bluff), corn and flour-mill, steam-power, owned by Alexander Kerr; corn and flour-mill, steam-power, owned by F. P. Jones; saw-mill, steam-power, owned by Henry Taylor. Still-houses were numerous from the very early days of the settlement until the breaking out of the civil war. The distilleries were long, low, log houses, and were supplied with the old-fashioned copper worm. The beer would be run off one day, allowed to cool for a day, and then run through the worm again on the third day. The capacity of the average still was about one barrel per day. Stills were owned by Hudson Johnson on Barton's Creek, by John Adams on Yellow Creek, by Christopher Strong and Daniel Leach on Johnson's Creek, Abraham Caldwell on Barton's Creek, Minor Bibb on Turnbull Creek, and by John Talum, William Hogan and Lum Bruce in the First District. These were the early stills, from the first down to the last, in the order named.

There were no offices in Dickson County until the year 1806, when the first one was established at Charlotte, of which Richard Waugh was probably the first postmaster. Other early postmasters were Absolom Massie, Robert McNeiley and William James. The postoffices of the county at present are as follows: Second District, Hazel Ridge; Third District, Spencer's Mill; Fourth District, Burns and Larkins; Fifth District, Dickson and Colesburg; Sixth District, Charlotte and Cloverdale; Seventh District, Bellsburgh; Eighth District, Cumberland Furnace and Bufrange; Ninth District, Wood's Valley; Tenth District, Batson's Store; Eleventh District, Cave Mill, Danielsville and Dull; Twelfth District, White Bluff; Thirteenth District, Gillam. The principal slave owners of Dickson County were as follows: Anthony W. Vanlier owned about 100; Montgomery Bell, 200; Dr. E. W. Napier, 50; Henry Napier, 40; George Napier, 75; Joab Hardine, 30; Benjamin and Theodrick Collier, 50; William S. Fentress, 100, and Thomas McNeiley, 24.

In May, 1830, Dickson County was visited by a very destructive hurricane. The court house and jail at Charlotte were demolished. The books and papers in the former building were scattered in every direction for miles, and many of them entirely destroyed. Several large books were carried by the wind into Cheatham County, and afterward recovered. A man was in the second story of the court house when the storm occurred, and was completely buried in the rubbish, but escaped serious injury. The roof of the jail was carried over thirteen miles. Charlotte was damaged by this storm to the extent of about $30,000, and the balance of the county as much more.

Dickson County has a population of nearly 14,000, of which there were 2,700 voters at the 1884 election, nearly five-sixths being Democrats. In 1855 the population was 8,404, of which number 6,286 were white, and 2,118 slaves. Financially the county is in an excellent condition, it being entirely free from debt and its orders selling at par. The tax levy on the $100 for the present year is as follows: County purposes, 30 cents; school, 20 cents; road, 10 cents. The total number of acres in the county assessed for taxation, in 1885, was 283,511, and the total value of real and personal property assessed at $859,480, while the total taxes amount to $12,966. The Nashville, Chattanooga & St. Louis Railway (St. Louis division) passes through the county east and west, and the Nashville & Tuscaloosa Railway has its northern terminus at Dickson, but from neither road does the county derive any revenue, as by their charters each road is exempt from taxation for the period of twenty years from the date of their completion, and that date will not expire until 1888. In 1885 there were 3,760 horses and mules in Dickson County, 7,970 cattle, 5,640 sheep and 22,670 hogs. The cereal products of the county in the above year were barley, 30 bushels; buckwheat, 117 bushels; corn, 616,422 bushels; oats, 50,735 bushels; rye, 555 bushels; wheat, 45,318 bushels.

Dickson County is bounded north by the counties of Houston and Montgomery, east by Cheatham and Williamson, south by Hickman and west by Humphreys and Houston. The county was named in honor of William Dickson, of North Carolina, who was a United States surveyor. The county was erected out of the counties of Robertson and Montgomery October 25, 1803, by the following enactment:

AN ACT ERECTING PART OF ROBERTSON AND MONTGOMERY COUNTIES INTO A SEPARATE AND DISTINCT COUNTY.

SECTION 1. Be it enacted by the General Assembly of the State of Tennessee, That a new county by the name of Dickson be, and hereby is erected and established out of that part of Robertson and Montgomery comprehended within the bounds following, to wit: Beginning on the south bank of Cumberland River, where the line which separates the counties of Robertson and Davidson intersects the same, running thence down said river to a point half a mile below Fayetteville; thence southwardly to a line which shall intersect Barton's Creek, one-half mile north of the forge; thence due west to a stake or point one (1) mile east of the east boundary line of Stewart County; thence south to the southern boundary of this State; thence east with said southern boundary to the southwest corner of Williamson County, as established by an act of the last session of the General Assembly, entitled "An Act to extend the jurisdiction, and to ascertain the bounds of the counties therein mentioned;" thence north with the west boundary lines of the counties of Williamson and Davidson, to the beginning.

The above limits were materially reduced by an act of the Legislature, passed December 3, 1807, which provided for the establishment of Hickman County out of the south part of Dickson, and again by an act creating Humphreys County, passed October 19, 1809, and again in the erection of Cheatham County, by an act passed February 22, 1856, and still again by an act passed January 23, 1871, by which a portion of the county was taken in the formation of Houston County. The county at present contains 470 square miles. Section 2 provided that the first court of pleas and quarter session should be held by the justice at the dwelling house of Robert Nesbitt, on Barton's Creek, the first Monday in February next Section 3 provided for holding elections and musters. Section 4 provided that the sheriffs of Robertson and Montgomery Counties should collect taxes in the respective parts stricken off for the ensuing year, and tax arrearages for preceding years. Section 5 appointed James Elder, surveyor, to run the line between the counties of Montgomery and Dickson, and authorized him to hire assistants, the expense to be paid by Dickson County. Section 6 made Dickson County part of the electoral district to which Robertson and Montgomery Counties belonged. Section 7 provided that the sheriffs of Robertson, Montgomery, Stewart and Dickson Counties should meet at Clarksville the Monday succeeding elections, to compare the rates, and that the sheriff of Robertson County should certify the poll for governor, representative to congress and representatives to the General Assembly for the counties of Robertson and Dickson.

By a supplemental act, passed November 7, 1808, the sheriff of Dickson County was directed to hold an election the first Thursday in June, and the succeeding day, at the place of holding courts, to elect field officers for the county; and the justices in that part of Dickson stricken from Montgomery County were authorized to continue their duties in the new county. By an act passed August 8, 1804, Robert Dunning, Sterling Brewer, John Davidson, Montgomery Bell and George Clark were appointed commissioners to fix on the most central and suitable situation for the erection of a court house, prison and stocks for Dickson County, whose duty it was to purchase forty acres of land on the most reasonable terms, on some part of which the above buildings were to be erected. The commissioners were also authorized to lay off the said forty acres into a town, to be called Charlotte, and to sell said town lots, and with the proceeds of such sales erect and pay for the court house, prison and stocks, and should the money derived from such sales be insufficient to pay all the costs incurred in erecting such buildings, the county court was authorized to levy a tax for such purchase. Pursuant to the above act Montgomery Bell, William Doak, William Russell, Sterling Brewer, Gabriel Allen, William Teas, Lemuel Harvey, Jesse Croft and Richard C. Napier, the justices provided for by said supplemental act, met and qualified on Monday, March 19, 1804, at the residence of Col. Robert Nesbitt. The house in which the first session of the county court was held remains standing in very good repair, being occupied by a grandson of Col. Nesbitt. It is a one-story log building, and stands about three miles north of the county seat. After appointing Robert Drake, clerk *pro. tem.*, and Drury Christian, sheriff *pro. tem.*, the court adjourned over until 11 o'clock the next day, when it again met, and there being a full attendance of justices the following officers were elected to serve until the next regular election should be held. Clerk, Daniel Dickson; sheriff, Benjamin Weakley; register, James Walker; commissioner of revenue, Robert Drake; county trustee, John Larkins; wood ranger, William Caldwell; coroner, John Hall; all of whom were qualified and entered upon the discharge of their official duties. One of the first acts of the court was to appoint Ezekiel Norris, general, and James Fentress special guardian of John Davis, son of John Davis, deceased, and to order a road laid off leading from Yellow Creek to the Montgomery County line, on the middle fork of Barton's Creek.

The following jury was appointed to serve at the following June court of pleas and quarter sessions; John Burton, Redner Adams, William Brasier, William Runland, Howel Adams, Andrew Giffin, Robert Nesbitt, Thomas Simpson, Samuel Walker, Simeon Walker, James Ross, Lewis Russell, John Larkins, Jr., Robert

Stington, John Ward, Moses Smith, Nathan Nesbitt, Hugh Robertson, Samuel Hartly, Matthew Gilmore, Edward Lucas, Cornelius Magraw, Andrew Caldwell, Burgess Harris, John Holland, Robert Norris, William Moore, Samuel Parker, Thomas Mitchell, James Woods, Earl Hutchen, Thomas Napier, Stephen Ward, Levi Hand, Michael Dickson, William McKnight, Charles Walker and John Davidson, and out of the above a grand jury of fourteen and a foreman were selected at the meeting of court.

At the June term of the county court the prices regulating the Harpeth River ferry, were established. For man and horse, 12 ½ cents; single horse 6 ¼ cents; footman, 6 ¼ cents; sheep and hogs per head, 1 ¼ cents; wagon and team, $1; two-wheel carriages, 50 cents; cattle per head, 6 ¼ cents. Indictments were returned by the grand jury at this term as follows: David Ross, rescuing; William Carrin, trespass and assault and battery; John Craft, assault and battery.

From the year 1808 until the year 1815 there are no records to show the proceedings of the county court, but during that time the commission appointed by the said act carried out the instructions contained therein and selected a county site at what is now Charlotte. The land was owned by Charles Stewart, who, in 1808, donated fifty acres to the commission upon which to locate the county site, and lay off a town, which was christened Charlotte. Upon being platted the lots were sold to the highest bidders, and with the money derived from the sale the public buildings were erected. Just when these buildings were completed cannot at this late day be ascertained, as the records of the county court between the years 1808 and 1817 have been lost or destroyed. However, it was some time between 1810 and 1812 that the buildings were finished and moved into. The court house, a large substantial brick, was erected at a cost of between $10,000 and $12,000. It was square in shape, two stories in height, the county offices being below on the first floor, and the whole of the second floor being used as a court room. There were four entrances to the building, all opening into a large hall. A large circular belfry surmounted the roof. The jail was also a two-story brick building, being also a sheriff's residence, and cost about $4,000. Both the court house and jail were destroyed by the storm of 1830, but were rebuilt by the county court, during the following year, in the same places and in the same style and manner, and at about the same cost. The sessions of the court were held in the public school house until the new buildings were erected Peter Seals was the first man sent to the State prison from Dickson County, and he was sent there by the county court in 1830, for whipping his wife.

Previous to 1836 the poor of the county were kept by different individuals in the separate civil districts, at the expense of the county, appropriations being made from time to time by the county court. In the above year the court passed an order for the purchase of ground and the erection of necessary buildings to be used as a county asylum. The ground was purchased at a point about two miles from Charlotte, on the Dickson road, upon which was erected a comfortable log house, at a cost of about $400; the house was found to be inadequate of recent years, and in 1870 the court passed another order for the sale of the property, and for the purchase of a suitable tract of land situated four miles from Charlotte, on the Nashville road, upon which were erected a number of small log houses for the accommodation of the overseer and paupers. The land and buildings cost upward of $25,000.

A bit of interesting history was enacted by the county court in 1833, which has few precedents in the State of Tennessee. It was as follows: On the 25th of November, 1833, William C. Bird, a white man and a patrol, was assaulted by one Wiley, a slave, with a club and murdered. Wiley was soon afterward arrested, and the county court convened in special session on the 19th of December of the same year for the purpose of trying the slave on the charge of murder. The trial was by jury, and lasted three days, a verdict of guilty being returned on the third day, fixing the penalty at death by hanging. The charge was read to the negro, and the day of his execution being set for December 28, following, he was remanded to jail. On the appointed day Wiley was taken from jail and placed in a cart and conveyed to the place of execution. The gallows had been erected the previous day at a point about half a mile east of Charlotte, and was in the shape of two upright posts and a cross piece, to which the rope was attached. Several thousand people gathered on the surrounding hillsides and climbed up into the neighboring trees to witness the hanging. Slave owners took their slaves to see the negro hung, hoping thereby to give them a terrible lesson and warning. The cart bearing the doomed man was driven between the two uprights, the noose was placed around the slave's neck, and the driver was instructed to "drive up the cart," and the negro was jerked into eternity. An aged darkey preached a funeral sermon over the remains, and delivered a solemn warning to his brethren.

In 1836 the State Legislature passed an act creating the circuit court, and one reorganizing and reconstructing the county courts of the State. Previous to this time the county court had jurisdiction in any and all cases, both criminal, civil and probate. But by the requirements of this act of the Legislature, the jurisdiction of the county court was limited to county affairs, the circuit and chancery court being given jurisdiction over all cases of justice and equity. The county court clerks have been as follows from the organization of the county to the present: David Dickson, from

1804-13; Fiel Farrar, 1813-36; William Hightower, 1836-42; Thomas J. Kelley, 1842-43; Thomas McNeiley, 1843-59; Thomas C. Morris, 1859-65; F. M. Binkley, 1865-70; Thomas K. Grigsby, 1870-86, and is a candidate for re-election.

From some time during the year 1819 until about 1821 or 1822, the Supreme Court of the State of Tennessee held regular sessions at Charlotte. The records of this court, or at least of its sessions held in Charlotte, have been lost, and as there are no citizens whose memory is clear on the subject, it is impossible to give any account of the proceedings. The judges were three in number, and were probably Haywood, Emmerson and Catron.

The Circuit Court of Dickson County, in common with similar courts throughout the State, was established by an act of the Legislature of Tennessee passed January 25, 1836. By this act Dickson County was placed in the Seventh Judicial District, of which Hon. Mortimer A. Martin was judge, and William K. Turner was attorney-general. Previous to that time the county court had full jurisdiction in all cases, both criminal and civil. During the war of the Rebellion the records of the circuit court were damaged and destroyed to a considerable extent, and of the first three years' proceedings of the court there is now no record, the dockets and minute books being entirely lost. The first session of the court, of which there is a record was held in the court house at Charlotte, beginning on the second Monday of June, 1839, over which Judge Martin presided. The first grand jury, of which there is a record, also met at this term of court, and was composed of the following gentlemen: Willie Bothrop, John S. Spencer, William Willey, David Frazier, William White, Jesse Graham, Elisha Lloyd, James Loggins, Lawson Gunn, Thomas McMurry, Josiah Ferrill and Berryman S. Walker, of which Willie Bothrop was chosen foreman. Among the indictments returned by this grand jury were one against Warren Hill for drunkenness, and James Bruce for assault and battery. Jesse Norris was convicted of grand larceny at the February term, 1842, and sent to the penitentiary for three years. At the February term, 1843, Richard Hutson was sent to the penitentiary for three years on the charge of horse stealing. At the June term of the same year Henry D. James was sent to the county jail for one hour on being convicted of the charge of rescue. Aaron D. Cochran was convicted of usury at the February term, 1844, and fined $25, while at the following term William H. Nichols and William Baker were tried and acquitted of the charge of murder.

From the October term, 1845, until the June term, 1855, the records are missing. At the latter date John Luther was sent to the penitentiary for four years for harboring slaves, Scarborough Penticost was acquitted of the charge of killing of one Edwards, and the entire family of Samuel H. Moran, including himself, wife and four children, were bound over to keep the peace for twelve months, each one being required to give $500 bond.

Willis Johnson was tried and convicted of the murder of John Welsh at the February term, 1857, and sent to the penitentiary for six years. P. H. Hamilton was convicted of forgery at the February term, 1859, and sent to the penitentiary for three years, and at the following term Sanford Higgs, Henry and Andrew Elridge were convicted on the double charge of murder and arson and each sent to the penitentiary for fifteen years. At the October term, 1861, John H. and W. J. H. Ross and D. A. Gallighy were convicted of murder in the first degree and sentenced to be hung. Their case was taken to the supreme court at Nashville, and the prisoners were liberated by the Federal soldiers when that city was captured during the war. Beginning with May, 1862, the circuit court transacted little or no business for several terms, and were finally abandoned and were not opened again until after the close of the war, when the first session was held in June, 1866. At that term Thomas Smith was sent to the penitentiary for stealing a hog. At the February term, 1867, Willis Holt and Wesley Hood were each sent to the penitentiary for fifteen years for stealing a horse. Betty Nixon was convicted of grand larceny at the October term, 1868, and sent to the penitentiary for one year. Nathan Bowan, colored, was convicted of the murder of Robert Collins at the June term, 1870, and sent to the penitentiary for ten years. Samuel Porter was convicted of the murder of Jack Snowden at the March term, 1871, and sent to the penitentiary for ten years, and at the following July term Henry White was sent to the penitentiary for life for the murder of Stanford Donnegan. At the March term, 1876, Jesse Dowing, colored, was sent to the penitentiary for sixteen years upon a charge of ku-klux. William Still was sent to the penitentiary for three years on the charge of grand larceny at the July term, 1879, and was tried and convicted on the same charge at the March term, 1880, and sent back for three years more. Andrew White was tried at the March term, 1881, on the charge of larceny and sent to the penitentiary for sixteen years, and at the following term White was tried on the charge of murdering James Clardy and was convicted and sentenced to be hung, but his sentence was commuted by the governor to imprisonment in the penitentiary for life. At the March term, 1885, Warren Bishop was sent to jail for ten days for committing manslaughter, and at the following November term Jeff Clark was sent to the penitentiary for ten years for murder, and John Grace was convicted of the murder of D. W. Price and sent to the penitentiary for five years.

The following is a list of the officers of the Dickson County Circuit Court from the organization of the court to the present time: Judges— Mortimer A. Martin, from 1836-52; W. W. Pepper from 1852-61; Thomas W. Wisdom from 1861 to the breaking out of the war, and presided over the first term of court after civil law was restored in 1865; John Alex. Campbell from 1865-69; James E. Rice from 1869-78; Joseph C. Stork from 1878 until the present time, and is the present incumbent. Attorney-generals— William K. Turner from 1836-42; W. B. Johnson, 1842-48; V. S. Allen, 1848-50; J. M. Quarles, 1850—58; W. E. Lowe, 1858-62, James E. Rice, 1865-69; W. J. Broaddus, 1869-70; T. C. Milligan, 1870-78; B. D. Bell, 1878 until present time. Clerks—John C. Collier, 1836-42; Robert McNeiley, 1842-62; James E. Justice, by appointment, 1865-66; H. C. Collier, 1866-70; J. A. Dodson, 1870-86. Dickson County is now in the Tenth Judicial District, which is composed of the counties of Robertson, Montgomery, Dickson, Stewart, Sumner and Houston. Many eminent lawyers practiced before the Charlotte bar between the thirties and sixties; men who made their mark as jurists, statesmen and politicians. Among the local lawyers of the above period were John C. Collier, W. H. Dortch, John Montgomery, John Reed, S. L. and James Finley, Robert and Thomas McNeiley, Lucien B. Chase and A. G. Williams, all of whom ranked well in their profession. The attorneys of the present are Thomas Morris, Jacob Leach, W. L. Grigsby and Hardin Leach.

The Chancery Court of Dickson County was established by an act of the General Assembly in 1836, but was held in Clarksville, Montgomery County, until October, 1737, at which time the court and records were removed to Charlotte, and the first session held in June of the following year, which was presided over by Judge Hamilton, chancellor of the Twelfth Chancery District. Judge Hamilton was succeeded by Judge Andrew McCampbell, who served until 1846 and was succeeded at that time by Judge

Jesse H. Cahal. Judge Cahal served until 1850; Judge A. O. P. Nicholson from 1850-51; Judge John S. Brien from 1851-54; Judge Samuel D. Frierson from March, 1854, to October, 1854; Judge Stephen Pavatt from 1854-66; Judge R. H. Rose from 1866-68; Judge J. W. Doherty from 1868-71; Judge G. H. Nixon, from 1871-86, and is the present incumbent and candidate for reelection. Chancery clerks and masters have served as follows: William A. Dortch, 1837-39; John C. Collier, 1839-54; Henry C. Collier, 1854-66; R. M. Baldwin, 1866-71; Henry C. Collier, 1871-81; W. L. Grigsby, 1881 to the present time, and has five years more of his term yet to serve.

The other county officers of Dickson County who have served since its organization: Sheriffs—Robert Weakley, 1804-06; David Hogan, 1806-08; Michael Malton, 1808-10; Edward Pearsall, 1810-11; James Read, 1811-13; Drury Christian, 1813-19; Richard Batson, 1819-25; David McAdoo, 1825-26; William Hightower, 1826-28; George Smith, 1828-35; Robert Livingston, 1835-38; George W. Tatum, 1838-40; Thomas McMurry, 1840-46; W. J. Mathis, 1846-52; W. L. White, 1852-53; G. W. Clarke, 1853-54; J. W. Hutton, 1854-60; John V. Walker, 1860-61; Eli Wylie, 1861-65; M. G. Harris, 1865 (served only two weeks); W. G. McMahan, 1865-66; D. L. Matlock, 1866-72; J. W. Hutton, 1872-77; W. M. Kirk, 1877-82; Rufus Ferfee, 1882-84; S. M. Grigsby, 1884-86, and the present incumbent and is a candidate for re-election. County registers—James Walker, 1804-16; Malton Dickson, 1816-23; Richard Waugh, 1823-42; Henry A. Bibb, 1842-48 ; L. L. Leach, served one month in 1848; E. E. Larkins, 1848-56; J. P. Priestly, 1856-60; E. E. Larkins, 1860-74; Henry A. Bibbs, 1874-86, and is the present incumbent and candidate for re-election. County surveyors—Thomas Williams, 1824-29; Malton Dickson, 1829-33; Sellman Edwards, 1833-45; David Gray, 1845-51; Willis Roberts,

1851-52; Sellman Edwards, 1852-54; Peter Jackson, 1854-58; A. Myatt, 1858- 69; Peter Jackson, 1869-73; Robert Martin, 1873-85; W. G. McMillan, 1885-86, and is the present incumbent. State senators—Duncan Stewart, 1805-07; Parry W. Humphreys, 1807-09; John Shelby, 1809-11; James B. Reynolds, 1811-15; Robert West, 1815-17; Sterling Brewer, 1817-19; James R. McMeans, 1819-21; Sterling Brewer, 1821-23; Robert Weakley, 1823-29; Henry Frey, 1829-31; Bowling Gordon, 1831-33; Thomas Shaw, 1833-39; J. B. Hardwick, 1839-41; Jacob Voorhies, 1841-45; Thomas Shaw, 1845-47; Stephen C. Paratt, 1847- 51; Samuel B. Moore, 1851-53; W. C. Whitthorne, 1858-57; Thomas McNeily, 1857-61; Joshua B. Frierson, 1861-67; Jesse E. Eason, 1867-69; W. A. Moody, 1869-73; Mitchell Trotter, 1873-75; H. M. McAdoo, 1875-77; Vernon F. Bibb, 1877-81; D. B. Thoruss, 1881-85, and present incumbent. Representatives—John Coleman, 1809-11; Sterling Brewer, 1811-13; William Easley, 1813-17; Robert C. Daugherty, 1817-19; Abraham Caldwell, 1819-21; Malton Dickson, 1821-23; Richard Batson, 1823-27; John Reed, 1827-31; Bowling Gordon, 1831-33; George Smith, 1833-35; Robert McNeiley, 1835-37; John Eubanks, 1837-47; William A. Moody, 1847-55; W. J. Mathis, 1855-57; F. T. V. Schmitton, 1857-59; William L. White, 1859-65; A. D. Nicks, 1865-67; M. J. J. Cagle, 1867-69; A. D. Nicks, 1869-73; Jacob Leach, 1873-75; J. J. Pollard, 1875-77; Jacob Leach, 1877-79; G. W. McQuary, 1879-83; W. J. Mallory, 1883-84; H. H. Buquo, 1884-85; N. B. Sugg, present incumbent.

The soldiers furnished by Dickson County to the war of 1812 were as follows: John B. Walker, Thomas Edwards, David McAdoo, William James, Benjamin Swift, Daniel Williams, James Bell, Thomas Williams, James Daniels, Thomas Gilbert, William Porter, John Jones, John Hall, John Tilley, William Dodson, James

Hightower, Obediah Spradlin, Abraham Heath, Simon Deloach, Jesse Beck, Francis Hunter, Drury Atkins, A. Etherage, Isaac Heath, Aaron Parrish, Willis Willey, Thomas Nesbitt, Richard Batson, Isaac Hill, David Bibb, Allen Bowen, Richard Watkins, Lansom Gunn, Anderson England and Edward Niblack. Those who went from Dickson County into the Florida war of 1836, in Capt. James Tatum's company, were Alexander Jones, Moses Street, Abraham Street, Allen Nesbitt, Mortimer Edwards, Joseph Parrish, William Tatom, James Hudgins, James Young, Hudson Shropshire, John Linke, Washington Weems and William Young. When the call was made for volunteers to serve in the Mexican war, in 1846, Dickson County responded promptly by raising two full companies, but before they could report at Nashville, Tenn., the quota was already full, and they were rejected. However, several members of the companies succeeded in getting into the service, and served throughout the war. They were W. J. Mallory, James Hudgins, William Tate, John Owens, Bass Ferrell and John Morris.

The part taken by Dickson County in the war of the Rebellion was a conspicuous one. She not only furnished her quota of soldiers to the Confederate Army, but was the scene of stirring events during the four years in which the war was waged. Until President Lincoln issued his call for 75,000 volunteers the people of Dickson County were rather disposed to remain passive and, if possible, maintain a neutral position on the question of secession. But the call to take up arms against the people of the South served to ignite a spark of indignation in their breasts, and the refusal of Gov. Harris was received by them with demonstrations of pleasure. Preparations were at once inaugurated for the raising and equipment of the county's quota of State troops, and in the first part of May following the first company was equipped and started for Nashville, under command of Capt. William Green. Two days later two more companies were started for the same destination, under command of Capts. W. J. Mallory and William Thedford. The companies were assigned places in the Eleventh Tennessee Regiment, being designated by letters C, H and K, in the order of captains given above. They were then sent to Camp Cheatham, in Robertson County, for instructions.

Upon another call made for volunteers, during the same year, two more companies were organized and equipped, and left in December following, under command of Capts. Thomas H. Grigsby and J. B. Cording; for Fort Donelson, where they were assigned to the Forty-ninth Tennessee Regiment, as Companies B and D, respectively. At different times during the war the Southern Army was recruited from among the citizens of the county; they going out in small squads and joining different commands. After a month spent in drilling, at Camp Cheatham, Companies C, H and K were ordered on post duty on the railroad between Hainsville and Knoxville. Under Gen. Zollicoffer they next went to Rock Castle, Ky., and participated in the battle of Fishing Creek, on the morning of the 19th of January, 1862, that being their first engagement. Their next engagement was at the siege of Cumberland Gap and next at the battle of Murfreesboro, December 31, 1862. The battles of Chickamauga, Mission Ridge, the memorable retreat from Dalton to Atlanta, Franklin, Nashville and the march to North Carolina were also participated in by the Dickson County boys. They were surrendered to Gen. Sherman April 9, 1865. Companies B and D, as above stated, went from Dickson County to Fort Donelson, where they experienced their initiative fighting. After the surrender the members of the two companies were taken to Alton, Ill., where the officers and men were separated, the former being taken to St. Louis, then to Camp Chase, Ohio, and next to Johnson's Island, while the latter were sent to Camp Douglas, Chicago, Ill., all being held as prisoners of war. The sketch of their service appeals elsewhere in this volume. At the final surrender of the army there remained but one man of Company B, William H. Taylor.

In 1862 a party of about sixty Federal soldiers visited the county on a raid, and a slight skirmish occurred between them and a band of guerrillas a few miles out from Charlotte, in which no damage was sustained by either side. During the latter part of November, 1863, a portion of two Federal regiments, numbering between 300 and 400, took possession of Charlotte. They were under command of Maj. Kirwine, and remained in Charlotte until the middle of March, 1864. They established headquarters in the court house, and erected barracks all around the court yard, and christened the same as "Camp Charlotte." During those months much damage was done to the town in addition to "eating the citizens out of house and home." The records in the court house were mutilated and destroyed in an inexcusable and wanton manner, and private and business houses invaded and pillaged. A continuous fight was kept up between the Federals and guerrillas, and not a few lives were sacrificed as a result. In 1864 William D. Willey was captured by the Federals under Lieut. Donnehue, and shot as a guerrilla. The latter, it is supposed, killed John Lindsey, a Federal sympathiser, during the same year, and in a short time thereafter Demps Dobson, a guerrilla, was captured by the Federals, and taken about a mile north of Charlotte and shot. When friends of the dead man went after the body to give it decent burial, they found in his hand a scrap of paper, on which was written, "Shot in retaliation for the killing of John Lindsey." M. Gilbert, a citizen of Charlotte, was also killed by the Federals. The Nashville, Chattanooga & St. Louis Railway (then known as the Northwestern

Railway) was guarded by detachments of Federals stationed at White Bluff, Burris' Station, Cox Springs and Gillam Station. The Federal Army had a large amount of stores and a considerable number of soldiers at Johnsonville, on the Tennessee River, in 1864, about the time Gen. Hood was moving on Nashville, and Gen. Forrest was dispatched to undertake their capture. The Federal troops no sooner learned the movements of that General than they were off for Nashville in hot haste. They reached Charlotte in a state of demoralization, having left behind them a trail marked by guns, ammunition, blankets, flour, meal, meat and in fact everything they found unhandy to carry in their flight. After passing through Charlotte and proceeding a mile or two they received word that Gen. Forrest had gotten between them and Nashville. This was the signal for retreat, and all moved rapidly to Clarksville.

Nothing, comparatively, can now be learned of the religious condition and happenings in Dickson County prior to the year 1800. At that time the Methodists, Baptists and Presbyterians had organizations in the county, though no church houses had been erected, and services, when held, were conducted in private residences, or during the pleasant weather season in some shady grove. Probably the first church erected in the county was a log building, which stood about half a mile west of where Charlotte now stands, and which was built some time in 1804 by the Psalm Singers, who, sometime before, led by the Rev. Samuel Brown, had seceded from the Presbyterian Church. The Psalm Singers were few in number, and, as an organization, did not live long in this county, and a grave-yard now marks the spot where once stood their church building.

The history of the Cumberland Presbyterian Church in Dickson County must always abound with interest, as that denomination, now prominent and flourishing in every State of the Union, had its origin in this county, in a log house, the home of Rev. Samuel McAdoo. The house in which was planned and organized the Cumberland Presbyterian Church stood about six miles south of Charlotte, and was an old-fashioned double log house, a story and a half high, which was covered with clapboards, the boards being held in place by weight poles. The chimneys were made of wood and dirt. The logs were hewn with a broad ax, and the cracks daubed with mud. The windows were small, and not being provided with glass were closed by clapboard shutters, hung with wooden hinges. In 1800 a great revival swept over portions of Kentucky and Tennessee, during which great numbers of sinners were converted to the religious belief, and the membership of the Presbyterian Church was increased tenfold. The organization of the Cumberland Presbyterian Church was one of, if not the greatest, results of this revival. The great increase in membership of the old church caused by the revival made the establishment of more churches and ordaining of new ministers a necessity, and although there were many able and pious men among the new preachers, the mother church refused to ordain them because of their lack of education, they not being possessed of a regular collegiate and classic education, and also because of their unsoundness of faith respecting the doctrines of election and predestation. They were also objected to on the ground of being too noisy in their meetings, they believing and practicing the revival system of securing conversions to the church. After a period of contention and dissatisfaction lasting several years a separation was effected. February 3, 1810, Revs. Fines Ewing, Samuel King and Samuel McAdoo, all regularly ordained ministers of the Presbyterian Church, met at the residence of the latter (in Dickson County), and after a night spent in prayer and consultation, on the following day formed a Presbytery, which was called the Cumberland Presbyterian Church. A few years afterward a church building was erected about four miles northwest of Charlotte, which was christened New Hope. This building was constructed of hewn logs, and is standing at the present time. The next church erected by the denomination was on Johnson's Creek, and stood about five miles northeast of Charlotte. During the thirties three more buildings were erected by the same denomination, they being Bethel Church on Yellow Creek, Bethlehem Church on Jones' Creek and Mount Liberty Church, situated on a ridge about twelve miles east of Charlotte. Rev. Gideon Blackburn, the able Southern preacher, and Rev. John L. Smith were among the most prominent of the ministers who occupied the pulpits of these early-day churches, and dispensed the teachings of religion to the early settlers.

Probably the first church erected by the Methodists was Smyrna Church, some time in 1810, which was a log building, and stood on Sulphur Fork of Jones Creek. The next was Mount Lebanon, also a log building, and stood about half a mile south of the first church. Mount Lebanon was rebuilt in 1880. During the thirties churches were erected by the Methodist denomination as follows: Mount Carmel, at the head of Barton's Creek; Soul's Chapel, on Horse Branch of Barton's Creek, and Bethany, on the Harpeth River. The early ministers of these churches were Revs. Michael Berry, who preached for sixty-two consecutive years; Rev. James Sizemore, Rev. Henry Hutton and Rev. Caleb Rucker.

The churches of the county by districts at the present time are as follows: First District—Eno Methodist Episcopal Church, South, on Piney River; Fewes Chapel, Methodist Episcopal Church, South, on Garner's Creek, and Oak Grove Methodist

Episcopal Church, North, situated between Garner's Creek and Piney River. Second District— Bethel, Baptist, and Beach Grove Methodist Episcopal, South, both on Piney River. Third District— Baptist, on Turnbull Creek; Box House, on Parker's Creek, at which meet both the Methodist Episcopal, North, and Missionary Baptist congregations. Fourth District—Grasses Spring Baptist, at Burn's Station; Marvin's Chapel, Methodist Episcopal Church, South, and Christian Church, both on Beaver Dam. Fifth District— One each of Methodist Episcopal, South, and Methodist Episcopal, North, United Baptist, Old School Presbyterian, Lutheran and two colored churches, one African Methodist Episcopal and one Methodist Episcopal, South. Sixth District—Fagan's Chapel, on Barton's Creek; Mount Carmel, on Barton's Creek; Sycamore, at head of Jones Creek; Mount Lebanon, on the Charlotte and Dickson Road; Liberty, on the Charlotte and Nashville Road; Green Brier, on the Harpeth Road, all Methodist Episcopal South; Big Spring, at head of Jones Creek; New Hope, at the head of the east prong of Barton's Creek, all Cumberland Presbyterians, and Bock House Christian, on Jones' Creek. At Charlotte, one each of Methodist Episcopal, South, and Cumberland Presbyterian, and also two colored churches, one each of African Methodist Episcopal and Baptist. Seventh District—Old Bethel, Methodist Episcopal, South, near mouth of Harpeth River; Mount Liberty, Cumberland Presbyterian, on a ridge near Harpeth River; Jackson's Chapel, Methodist Episcopal, South, and Brown's Chapel, Methodist Episcopal, South, both on Jones' Creek. Eighth District—St. James' Episcopal, at Cumberland Furnace, and Rock Spring Baptist, on Barton's Creek, and Soul's Chapel, Methodist Episcopal, South, one-half mile north of Cumberland Furnace. Ninth District—Liberty Methodist Episcopal, South, on Leatherwood Creek; Mount View Cumberland Presbyterian, between Barton's and Bear Creek; Valley Springs, Missionary Baptists, on

Barton's Creek, and Barton's Creek Church, Hard Side Baptists, on creek of that name. Tenth District—Stony Point, Cumberland Presbyterian, on Williamson Creek. Eleventh District —Wesley Chapel, Methodist Episcopal, South, at mouth of Cedar Creek; Union Methodist Episcopal, South, Maple Grove, Missionary Baptists, on west fork of Yellow Creek; Pleasant Hill Cumberland Presbyterian, on line between the Sixth and Eleventh Districts. Twelfth District—Two Methodist Episcopal, South Churches and one Cumberland Presbyterian Church at White Bluff; also a Colored Baptist and African Methodist Episcopal Church. Thirteenth District—One Methodist Episcopal Church, South, on Yellow Creek, and another of the same denomination on the Nashville, Chattanooga & St. Louis Railway.

Among the very early schools was one at the forks of Piney River, now in the Second District, which was taught by Alexander Campbell. The branches of instruction at the school consisted of reading, writing and spelling. The average attendance was about twenty-five scholars. Another similar school was conducted by James Scott, an Englishman, in the Hudson and Tatum neighborhood, now the First District. Mr. Scott was a thoroughly competent teacher and left a good record. Another school, on Turkey Creek, was taught by Jesse Boss, and still another on Piney River by Little John Donnegan. The first schools of any importance in the county were located at Charlotte, the first one of which was established some time in 1823. This school was conducted by Jacob Voorhies, of New Jersey, and was classical in its organization. Mr. Voorhies was followed by Robert Nesbitt, who conducted a very good school, but was not up to the standard of his predecessor, some time in 1827 or 1828. William James opened an excellent school in the vicinity of Charlotte, which was attended by scholars from all over the county. In 1830 a splendid school, known as Tracy Academy was established at Charlotte, and is in use up to the present day. Latin, Greek, and all the higher branches were taught at this school, and its pupils were not only from all parts of the county, but came from adjoining counties, and even other States. This school was supplied all along with excellent instructors, the first of whom was Prof. McGuiggin, Mrs. Richardson and then Miss Farley conducted the school, and in 1837 Prof. E. E. Larkins, the veteran school-teacher of Houston County, now teaching at Erin, taught for about a year, and was followed by Jesse Leigh, of New Hampshire. In 1839 Prof. Larkins again took the school in hand, and conducted it for two years. In 1840-43 J. R. Paschall taught the school, and was succeeded in 1843 by Prof. Larkins, who held the position of principal instructor until 1877. Rev. J. C. Armstrong, Prof. Larkin's assistant the previous year, succeeded to the professorship, and conducted the academy until 1880, at which time Mr. Larkin again assumed charge, and with Mrs. L. W. James, as assistant, conducted the institute until 1883. Since that time the school has been taught by Mrs. Bettie Dudley, of Kentucky. These schools were all in the nature of subscription schools, yet received assistance from the State. Some time in 1836, a first class private school was established and taught by Mr. W. B. Bell, on Barton's Creek, in what is now the Sixth District. This school established for itself a most excellent reputation, and was and is today patronized by students from all over the county. Mr. Bell, Sr., was succeeded by his son W. A. Bell, who conducts the school at present, under the name of Cloverdale Academy. Recently a first-class school, of the same nature as Cloverdale, has been opened under the name of Edgewood School, by Prof. Wade, assisted by his wife, Edgewood is on Yellow Creek, in the Eleventh District, and was opened in the spring of 1885. The Dickson Academy, an incorporated school, is also an excellent institute and is gaining a good reputation. This school was established in February, 1885.

The schools of Dickson County at the present time by districts are as follows: First District has 4 schools, all white; Second District, 4 schools, all white; Third District, 5 white schools and 1 colored; Fourth District, 6 white and 3 colored; Fifth District, 10 white and 3 colored; Sixth District, 8 white and 1 colored; Seventh District; 3 white and 3 colored; Eighth District, 7 white and 1 colored; Ninth District; 5 white and 1 colored; Tenth District, 5 white and 2 colored; Eleventh District, 5 white schools; Twelfth District, 6 white schools; Thirteenth District, 2 white schools. There are about 5,000 school children in the county, 4,000 of whom are white and 1,000 colored. The county superintendents have been as follows: L. L. Leach, 1873-77; T. F. McCreary, 1877-79: W. G. McMillan, 1879-84; B. F. Harris, present incumbent. Charlotte, the county seat of Dickson County, has about 400 inhabitants, and is situated very near the center of the county. It was laid off and platted in 1804. The land was owned by Charles Stewart, who donated it to the commission appointed to select a county site. The town contains fifty-nine lots, and is divided into blocks by eleven streets, running east and west and north and south. The surface of the town is very uneven, and is broken by deep ravines and washes. Town Branch, a tributary to Jones' Creek, flows through the town.

The first house, which was built of logs, was erected by William Peacock in the west part of the town some time during 1804, or probably before the town was platted. It remained standing until along in the fifties, when it was destroyed by fire. The next house erected stood on the southwest corner of the public square, and was built in about 1804 by John H. Hyde. This was also constructed of logs. Other houses followed, and by the year 1815 Charlotte was a live business town and growing rapidly. John Spencer was the first store-keeper; he opened up a combination establishment in 1806, in which he kept tavern and sold whisky, dry goods, groceries, and all kinds of provisions. Thomas Martin also conducted a similar establishment the year following, and during the same year Thomas Pannell, a hatter, opened up a shop and drove a brisk business in the manufacture and sale of woolen hats. The first cabinet and furniture shop was owned by Benoni Crawford, who made and sold all the furniture used in and around Charlotte. Elisha Williams was the village blacksmith from 1805 to 1808, and was followed by James Morris and Wilkin Corbin. Among the first citizens were William Peacock, Thomas Pannell, Elisha Williams, James Douglas, John H. Hyde, John Reed, Sterling Brewer, Benjamin Joslin, John Spencer. John Ellis, Marable Stone, Christian Robertson and Frank Ellis. The court house was built some time between 1810 and 1812, and destroyed by a storm in 1830 and was rebuilt in 1834. The first real tavern was established in 1810 by Frank Ellis. The building stood on the northwest corner of the public square, on what is now Col. T. K. Grigsby's garden patch, and opposite that gentleman's residence. In about 1812 Benjamin Joslin erected a large two-story tavern on the south side of the public square, and in doing so intended to improve the other buildings in regard to style. The old building remains standing at the present time, being used as a tenement house. It is a conspicuous feature of the town, its verandas and balcony catching at once the eye of a stranger on entering Charlotte. This tavern was under the proprietorship at different times, in the order given, of Christian Robertson, next by Benjamin Robertson, then Jonathan Hardwick, Thomas McNeiley, Mrs. Cording, and last by William Balthrop. The supreme court of the State held regular sittings in Charlotte during the years 1820-21, and the iron business being then in a flourishing condition, the town assumed an importance as a business center and trading point of which it cannot boast at the present. From 1820 to 1840 Charlotte enjoyed what would now be termed a "boom." By virtue of an act of the General Assembly, passed December 11, 1887, Charlotte was incorporated in the spring of 1838. Thomas Kelley was the first mayor elected, but of the other officers chosen at that election, nor of any proceedings of the town board from the incorporation of the town for quite a number of years, there remain no records. In fact until within a few years of the present there are no records, they all having been lost, burned or otherwise destroyed. The corporation is in force yet, with the following board of officers: mayor, Jacob Leach; recorder, T. H. W. James; marshal, W. E. Hicks; aldermen, C. C. Collier, T. C. Morris, T. H. W. James and W. E. Hicks.

The business men of the twenties were Christopher Robertson, Minor Bibbs, Thomas Pannell and Voorhies and Kelley, all of whom kept general merchandise. The business men of the thirties were all general merchants, and were John Ward, Jacob Voorhies, B. A. & T. M. Collier, William and James T. Massie. Business men of the forties were William Balthrop, Thomas Overton, Joab Harding and William James, all of whom kept similar stocks as their predecessors. Business men of the fifties were Leach & Dickson, W. C. Collier, William James, Thomas K. Grigsby, Thomas Overton and J. F. Davis, all being general merchants. The business men of the sixties, seventies and the present time are Mallory & Leach, general store, including drugs and bar-room; C. C. Collier, general store; W. C. Collier, same; Bowers and Sizemore, druggists; T. H. W. James, notions and stationery, also postmaster, and Abner Hickerson, groceries and bar-room. A first-class boarding house is conducted by Mrs. Martha Hickerson, and Joseph Taylor operates a blacksmith shop. Jacob Leach, T. C. Morris and Hardin Leach are the lawyers, and Dr. D. R. Leach and Dr. A. G. Castleman, the physicians.

The secret societies of Charlotte are Charlotte Lodge, No. 97, F. & A. M., which was organized and instituted October 6, 1842; Eureka Lodge, No. 813, K. of H., organized December 3, 1877, and Lily Lodge, K. & L. of H., organized March 26, 1880. The Masonic lodge was at one time very strong, but has been weakened in membership from time to time by the institution of the following lodges of the county, the members of which were taken from the parent lodge, No. 97; White Bluff Lodge, Dickson Lodge, Iron Lodge at Cumberland Furnace, Rainey Camp Lodge, McAllison Lodge and Yellow Creek Lodge. The memberships of both the lodges of K. of H., and K. & L. of H., are ordinarily strong. Charlotte has two good churches, the Cumberland Presbyterian and Methodist South, the former having a large brick church, which was erected directly after the close of the war, and the latter a substantial frame building. The membership of each is good. The colored people also have two church organizations, they being the African Methodist Episcopal and Baptists. One school is conducted in Charlotte, it being the old Tracy Academy, of which mention is made in full on another page. There is also a colored school taught in the public school season.

Dickson is by far the largest town in the county, and has about 1,000 inhabitants. It lies eight miles south of the county seat, and is situated on the Nashville, Chattanooga & St. Louis Railroad, and is also the northern terminus of the Nashville & Tuscaloosa Railroad. Being one of the best shipping points on the road a large amount of business is transacted by her many energetic business men. The town was laid off and platted by C. Berringer, of Allegheny City, Penn., the owner of the land, in the spring of 1868, though a railroad station was located on the present site of the town three years before. The first building in Dickson was erected during the war by W. H. Crutcher. It was a log house, and stood on the north side of the railroad crossing, where now is Main Street. Another log house was erected about the same time by Mr. Crutcher, which stood where J. R. Bryan's residence now stands, and was built for a store-room. Before completion both buildings were destroyed by the Federal soldiers, then encamped at Cox Springs nearby, and the material taken to that place and used in the construction of quarters for the troops. The first merchant of Dickson was Mr. Crutcher, who built a small log store, 16x16, during the latter part of 1865. The stock carried by Mr. Crutcher was of general merchandise, and his business was profitable, Other log houses were erected during the years of 1866-67, among which was one used as a tavern, which stood on what is now the corner of Main and Murrell Streets, opposite the Press office, and was conducted by C. J. Martin. The town continued to grow gradually, the buildings being erected in rapid succession, each one being on a more improved style of architecture than the preceding one, until at the present Dickson is an average size inland town, and has a bright future.

The merchants of the latter part of the sixties and the first part of the seventies were W. H. Crutcher, general store; McFarland & McCreary, same; J. C. Donnegan & Moore, same; Joseph McWilliams, same; A. Myatt, same; William Pickett, same; John Alexander, same; Miles H. Mayes, same; J. E. Spicer, same; W. H. Mathis, same; J. A. Thomas & Co., same; John Eickert, same; N. George, hardware; J. T. Henslee, drugs and general merchandise. The business men of the present are as follows: General merchants, John Rickert, J. E. Spicer, Murrell & Son, J. A. Thomas &

Co., W. J. Mathis, A. Myatt, Miller Bros., and E. L. Schmitton; drugs and general merchandise, Henslee & Coleman; hardware, tinware and furniture, Freeman & Cullum; fancy groceries, J. B. Bruce; harness, Aukney & McCaul; groceries, Mrs. Christ Nagley; boots and shoes, John Beckman and Robert Easley; tailors, Easley Bros.; jewelers, Bear & Dittis. Two good hotels are located in the town, under the management of Col. M. H. Mayes and Mrs. M. J. Mayes, respectively. Dickson also boasts of two first-class livery stables, the proprietors of which are Messrs. Hutton & Christian and W. J. Mathis; there are also two blacksmith shops, which are operated by Lee Shawl and Stroup & Lyttle; also two wagon manufactories, the proprietors being Joseph Davis and Sylvis & Best; the physicians are Drs. C. M. Lovell, B. Z. Henslee and G. W. Boyt; the first and only flour and corn-mill was erected in 1876 by Messrs. Nopp & Loafbourn, and is now owned by T. F. McCreary. The mill is a first-class steam mill in which is invested capital to the amount of $8,000. The educational facilities of Dickson are embraced in one school, the Dickson Academy, which was opened for the admission of scholars in February, 1885. It is a chartered school, and by its establishment Dickson was placed under the jurisdiction of the "four-mile law," by which the sale of liquor is prohibited. The churches of Dickson are seven in number—five white and two colored—and are as follows: Methodist Episcopal North, organized in 1867; Methodist Episcopal South, organized in 1872; United Presbyterian, organized in 1871; Old School Presbyterian, organized in 1869; Lutheran, organized in 1874, and the African Methodist Episcopal and Methodist Episcopal South (colored). The secret societies of Dickson are as follows: A. F. & A. M., removed to Dickson from Beach Grove in 1873; K. of H., organized in 1880; K. & L. of H., organized in 1883; G. T., organized in 1886; C. O. F., organized in 1881.

The only newspaper in the county is published at Dickson, and was established by its present publishers, Messrs. Conant & Freeman, in 1881, and has the appropriate name of *The Press*. This paper is a seven-column folio, and is gotten out in a neat and readable manner, and is conducted successfully, both financially and from a literary standpoint. The advertising patronage is liberal, while the circulation reaches 900, more than an average for a county newspaper. Previous to *The Press* the *Dickson County Independent* was conducted by N. B. Morton; that gentleman established *The Independent* in 1878, and continued its publication for three years. Dickson was incorporated in 1870, but the corporation was abandoned in 1883, and the records having became misplaced an account of the proceedings of the town board cannot be given. The town was originally called Smedsville, in honor of a civil engineer who located the first side-track at the place, but was subsequently changed to Dickson. The depot at Dickson is a handsome building, and is said to be the best on the railroad between Nashville and Chattanooga. Dickson is connected with Nashville, Burns Station and White Bluff by telephone.

White Bluff is a flourishing town of about 300 inhabitants, situated ten miles south of the county seat, and on the Nashville, Chattanooga & St; Louis Railway. The town takes its name from White Bluff Iron Forge, which at one time was in operation near the present site of the village. Probably the only good highway in the county passes through the town of White Bluff, the same being the old Charlotte & Nashville Pike. The town had its origin from having been a camp of the Federal soldiers during the war. Alexander Carr was the first man to locate in the town, he building a home for himself as soon as the soldiers departed from that vicinity. The first merchants were Morton & Wright, who opened a general store in 1865. The next merchants were Howell &

Crumpler, who setup in general merchandise business in 1867. The merchants following for the next ten years, all of whom kept general stores, including drugs, were George W. Collier, Charlton & Hicks, Jackson & Harris, F. E. Willey, John Hagie, and from that time to the present, J. G. Brown, C. Arnold and W. M. Beard, all of the above constituting the present merchants. The White Bluff Hotel is the only public hostelry, and is presided over by Mrs. Thomas Overton. White Bluff has three blacksmith and wagon shops, owned by S. H. Carson, Jones & Thompson, and John Luther. A planing-mill has recently been established by A. J. Carver & Co., which promises to add much to the town in the way of business. The railroad company has erected a neat depot. There is no school of a public nature taught immediately in White Bluff, as the school building was destroyed by fire in 1879, and has not as yet been rebuilt, though steps have been taken looking to the early erection of so important a building. Several good private schools constitute the educational advantages and facilities at the present.

The Southern Methodists, Cumberland Presbyterians and Christians have churches at White Bluff, also the colored Baptists and African Methodist Episcopal. White Bluff was platted in 1867 by A. Myatt, and incorporated in 1879. In 1882 the corporation was permitted to die out, and was renewed again in 1884. The corporation was again abandoned in 1885, in order to take advantage of the four-mile law, and a charter was obtained for a school, which was established near the town. White Bluff is surrounded by a splendid timber and farm country, and has quite a bright prospect ahead. In the amount of business transacted and as a shipping point it ranks close up to Dickson. The town is connected by telephone with Nashville, Dickson and surrounding towns.

Burns Station lies nine miles south of Charlotte, on the Nashville, Chattanooga & St. Louis Railway, and has a population of about 150. Upon the completion of the railroad, in 1860, Moses Tidwell, who owned the land where Burns now stands, erected a number of houses. These houses were afterward destroyed by the Federals during the war. The first man to engage in business at Burns was William Wadkins, who in 1868 established a general store. The following year Neiley & Stephens opened a store, and in 1870 were succeeded by Larkins & Son. In 1872 J. C. Donnegan purchased Mr. Wadkins' store, and in turn sold out to A. Myatt. In 1874 William Dowden opened a general store. Joseph Hendricks opened one in 1880, and J. C. Allspaugh one in 1881. Burns has one hotel, which is owned by F. F. Tidwell, T. K. Grigsby and W. M. Hogin, and one blacksmith shop, the property of A. D. Luther. Two lime works, of which mention is made elsewhere, are located one-half mile south of Burns. A chartered school, situated on Nail's Creek, serves both to educate the youth of Burns and also prohibit the sale of whisky in that section. The Primitive Baptists have the only church organization at Burns.

Gillam, or Tennessee City, is situated nine miles west of Dickson, on the Nashville, Chattanooga & St. Louis Railway, and has a population of about fifty people. Gillam Station was established upon the completion of the railroad, but was nothing more than a mere stopping place until in 1865, when Messrs. Pickett & Moody purchased several acres of land in the immediate vicinity of the station and erected a store-house, in which they sold general merchandise. The only other establishment at that time was a blacksmith shop owned by Jesse Haywood. In 1868 Daniel Rice opened a general store at Gillam, and is to-day the only merchant in the place. Messrs. Pickett & Moodey having dissolved and the latter dying, Mr. Haywood sold his blacksmith shop in 1870 to William

England, who ran the business for a few years and then abandoned it. The first physician who practiced at Gillam was Dr. W. A. Moodey, who was succeeded by Dr. William Bray, and he in turn by Dr. Oscar Moodey. In 1886 W. A. Schoenfeld, a Chicago capitalist, purchased a large tract of land lying on both sides of the railroad, and had the same laid out and platted into 20,117 town lots of fifty feet front, and gave the embryo city the name of Tennessee City. Whether the scheme of establishing a city at Gillam of the dimensions proposed by the projector will amount to anything remains to be seen. As yet it is a town on paper only. Gillam has a good railroad depot. Bon Air, or Colesburg, is another railroad station, and is situated two and one-half miles east of Dickson. Bon Air has about seventy-five inhabitants. The first business man was W. H. Crutcher, who began selling general merchandise in 1863. In 1879 Mr. Crutcher erected a large building, in which he opened a hotel, but did not continue in the hotel business long, and the building is now a dwelling house. J. C. Donnegan opened a store in 1870, but continued in business only a few years, selling out to F. C. Willey. The present merchant is J. D. Griffin. At Bon Air is located the sumac-mill of J. F. Gunkle, of which mention is made elsewhere. A saw and grist-mill is ran in connection with the sumac-mill. A neat depot has lately been erected here.

J. T. HENSLEE,

DICKSON COUNTY.

PART TWO

BIOGRAPHIES

William M. Adams was born in Roane County, East Tennessee, August 8, 1813, being the sixth of fourteen children born to Nelson and Martha (Mathis) Adams. The father was born in Hamilton County, Tenn., in September, 1813, and is still living in this county on the head waters of Yellow Creek. The mother was born in the year 1816. Our subject entered the Confederate Army at the age of nineteen years, joining Company G, Twelfth Tennessee Regiment, entering as second lieutenant and was afterward promoted to first lieutenant and in 1865 was made captain. At the close of the war he went west as a volunteer to fight the Indians. The following October he was discharged and came home. He entered the merchandise business with Jesse Daniels at Danielsville, but remained with him but a few years. He is a carpenter and built the Edgewood Schoolhouse. He was married, January 15, 1866, to Tennessee Dickson Daniel. She was born September 15, 1847. They have ten children: Jessie R., Bettie G., William W., Joseph A., Enola Ann, Emma A., Mattie L., Cora Hattie, Charley C. and Lewis Wade. Politically he is a Republican.

Isaac M. Bowers, a prominent merchant and tobacco dealer of Charlotte, is a native of Wilson County, Tenn., of which county his father, William W., was also a native. The mother was a native of Christian County, Ky., where the father married her. They settled in Wilson County and lived there till 1848, when they removed to Davidson County. In 1851 they made their home in Hopkins County, Ky., where the mother died in 1880 and the father in 1883. The subject of this sketch was born May 27, 1835, and was reared on a farm and secured a limited country school education. At the age of eighteen he went to Nashville, and for ten years clerked in a hotel. He then ran a billiard hall for three years. In 1861 he enlisted in Company K, First Kentucky Cavalry, in which he served one year, and then served in another company one year. After this he was one of the scouts for Gen. Forrest's command. Coming from the war he clerked in a hotel one year, then married and settled to farming in Kentucky for one year. In 1866 he went to Alabama and engaged in merchandising for three years. In 1869 he settled in Charlotte, where he has ever since run a general mercantile trade. He opened the tobacco trade in 1874; he was married, November 1, 1865, to Mrs. Mary C. Cayce, a daughter of Thomas McNeilly, of Charlotte. Five living children now bless this union: Maud, Julia, Horace J., Paul R. and Mary. He and his wife are members of the Cumberland Presbyterian Church. Politically he is a Democrat. He is highly respected as a valuable citizen of Dickson County.

Edward Brown, superintendent and general manager of the N. & T., Narrow Gauge Railroad, was born in Lynchburg, Va., June 11, 1834, being one of the family of seven brothers and three sisters of Edward and Martha Anne (Rucker) Brown. The father was a native of Birmingham, England. He was a watchmaker and jeweler, who lived and died in Virginia; his death occurred in 1851.

The mother was a native of Amherst County, Va., died in 1847. The immediate subject of this sketch was reared in Lynchburg, securing a common school education. At the age of seventeen years he served an apprenticeship in the machine shops on the old Virginia & Tennessee Railroad At the age of twenty he began running an engine on the same road and continued to do so steadily till 1869, when he engaged in same vocation on the East Tennessee & Georgia Road for ten months. From that time till 1879 he was engineer on the Nashville, Chattanooga & St. Louis Railroad. Since June 16, 1879, he has efficiently served his present trust to the complete satisfaction of all parties concerned. In 1856 he was united in marriage to Miss Susan W. Peters, of Sussex County, Va., the result of this union being one daughter, Edmonia P., now the wife of William S. Scott, of Dickson. This wife died in 1859. Mr. Brown then chose and wedded Anna McDaniel, of Lynchburg. This union has been blessed by a charming family of six children, viz.: Dollie W., Lizzie C., L. Leftwich, Alice H., Emma L. and John E. Capt. Brown and family are members of the Episcopalian Church. He is a member of the F. & A. M., K. of H., K. L. of H., A. O. U. W. and Good Templar organizations. Politically he is of old line Whig ancestry, and he himself cast his first presidential vote for John Bell; since the war has been a Democrat. He is too thoroughly known as a most valuable citizen of Tennessee, for us to do other than speak of him as a very moral, upright and energetic man, who has made success by diligent and steady application to his trust.

J. R. Bryan, bridge superintendent of Nashville, Chattanooga & St. Louis Railroad, is a native of Robertson County, Tenn., and was born August 12, 1844. He was the sixth of eleven children born to the marriage of W. P. P. C. Bryan and Malinda Lenox. The father was superintendent of the Sycamore Mills of Robertson County. He died in 1881. The mother died in 1858. At the age of fifteen J. R. entered Company E, Eighteenth Tennessee Volunteers, Confederate States Army. After the fall of Fort Donelson he was transferred to Forrest's cavalry brigade. A short time after coming from the war he began the carpenter's trade on bridges, and worked but seven days when he was promoted to foreman of a squad of men on bridge construction on the Northwestern Road. In February, 1870, he was promoted to his present trust, and now has entire charge of all bridges of the Nashville, Chattanooga & St. Louis and Northern & Tennessee lines of road. He is also engaged with J. A. Thomas in general merchandising in Dickson. He is senior member of J. R. Bryan & Co. in the manufacture of lime, staves, etc., and is merchandising at Burns' Station. He is also a member of the Dickson Oil Company. Since the date of his marriage, April 5, 1869, he has resided in Dickson. His wife was Anna M. Truby. This union has been blessed in the birth of five children, three of whom are now living, viz.: Maggie E., Mattie M. and Robert T. Mr. Bryan is a member of the F. & A. M. and K. of H. fraternities. He has always been a Democrat in politics. He is a very enterprising and successful business man.

Dr. W. C. Charlton, a worthy resident of White Bluff, was born January 9, 1831, being the fifth of six children born to John L. and Catherine B. (Pollard) Charlton, residents of Montgomery County, Va. The father was a very successful, wealthy and influential farmer and his brother, our subject's, uncle, was a member of the General Assembly of Virginia for twenty years. Our subject received but a limited education while with his parents, and at the age of thirteen years left the parental roof and served an apprenticeship in the wagon and carriage-making shop of J. A. Clay for three and a half years. He then followed his trade a number of years, and with the money he accumulated attended a medical college in Nashville, with Dr. W. Bollen as instructor, and graduated after a three years' course. During the first year of his attendance he was janitor of the building, and during the remainder of the time was assistant in chemistry. He practiced his profession two years in Ashland City, three years in Erin, and in 1869 removed to White Bluff, where he is a successful practitioner. The Doctor is literary in his tastes and his library is one of the most complete in the county. He was married, November 28, 1855, to Nancy Ann Troublefield. To them were born seven children, three of whom are living: Nannie L., Willie C. and George M. The family are members of the Methodist Episcopal Church South. Dr. Charlton is a member of the F. & A. M. and I. O. O. F., and he is a firm Democrat and stands high in the estimation of the people.

Winfield S. Coleman, a prominent young business man of Dickson County, came to Dickson at the age of twenty-two in the fall of 1880, and formed a partnership with J. T. Henslee in the drug and general merchandise trade, in which he has been very successful. He retired from this firm in the spring of 1886 to assume an interest in the firm of J. B. Bryan & Co. in the manufacture of lime, staves, etc. He was the third of a family of five children born to the marriage of Thomas J. and Priscilla (Lugg) Coleman. The father was a native of Dickson County and was born in 1826. He was a school-teacher and farmer and died in 1864. The mother is yet living in this county four miles north of Dickson. W. S. was reared on a farm with his parents to the age of twenty-two and received a very limited education. He is a thoroughly successful and entirely self-made man. He is a member of the Democratic party and a very highly respected citizen of the county.

William C. Collier, a prominent merchant of Charlotte, was the eldest of eight children born to the marriage of John C. Collier and Mary Clemments. John C. Collier was of English descent and was born in Virginia. When young he came to Tennessee, where he married the mother, who was of Scotch descent. The father was an attorney at law and died in Charlotte, in 1869, where he lived for fifty years. The mother died in 1843. At the age of eighteen years our subject engaged as clerk in a store, and in 1846 succeeded his employer and has continued the business till the present, except a short time during the war. He also owns 250 acres of land. He was married, in 1853, to Louisa B. Woodward, the fruits of this union being nine children, three of whom died in infancy and six now living, viz.: John E., William C., James G., Nancy C., Mary E. and Sallie B. Himself, wife and eldest daughter are members of the Cumberland Presbyterian Church. He was a Whig in politics before the war, but is now a Democrat and one of the oldest citizens of the county, his birth having been March 8, 1818, at Clarksville, Tenn. Christopher C. Collier, brother of the above, was born in Dickson County. At the age of twenty-two he began clerking and continued till 1865, with the exception of four years' service in Company C, Forty-ninth Tennessee Volunteers, Confederate States Army. He has been merchandising ever since 1865, and has been successful. Politically he is like his brother. Both these gentlemen are recognized as good and substantial citizens of Dickson County.

Joe Cox was born in Dickson County, Tenn., October 7, 1832, and is the eldest of five children born to William and Amelia (Brown) Cox. The father was born in this county and State in 1810, and the mother in Uniontown, Penn., in 1802. At the age of twenty years our subject went to Missouri, where he engaged in farming for four years, at the expiration of which time he went to California and engaged in teaming, mining and farming. After remaining there thirteen years he returned to Tennessee, in 1869, and engaged in farming, which occupation he still follows. In 1871 he took a trip through some of the Western States, but remained only a short time, when he returned. Politically he is a Democrat, and a man of good standing in his community.

James N. Cunningham was born in Dickson County, Tenn., February 24, 1864, being the son of Eliza and Harriet (Tally) Cunningham. The parents were natives of North Carolina. The father was a physician, having graduated at the medical college in Philadelphia in the year 1824. He practiced his profession in Dickson County until his death, which occurred in 1870. The mother is still living at the age of fifty-three years, making her home in Clarksville with one of her sons, she having three sons there who are engaged in the mercantile business. Our subject is about twenty-two years of age, and a young man of considerable energy. His life has been an eventful one, also one of hard labor. His father having died when he was but five years old, his educational advantages were rather limited, having received only a common school education. Practically he is a Democrat. His grandparents were some of the oldest pioneers of Tennessee.

Thomas S. Curtis was born at the old Cumberland Rolling-Mills, Stewart County, Tenn., July 26, 1855. His father was born at Spring Hill, Maury County, and at the age of fifteen began the manufacture of pig-iron. When eighteen years of age he was given the position of manager of the rolling-mills, which position he held until 1861, when he enlisted in the Southern Army. In the year 1866 he came to Cumberland Furnace, Dickson County, and assumed the duties of bank manager, which position he now holds. The mother died when Thomas S. was but nine years old. He was sent to school at Charlotte, then to Dickson, and from there to Union. He was then engaged as clerk five years for

Droullard & Co., at Cumberland Furnace, after which he attended school for a short period at Cloudale College, and leaving school he traveled for the Nashville Nurseries. He then returned to the furnace, where he was employed as book-keeper, which position he still holds. His marriage with Eudora Grimes was solemnized October 25, 1880. Five children have been born to them, all of whom are dead. He and wife are members of the Episcopal Church. In politics he is a Democrat, and is one of the most prominent men in this county.

Jesse Daniel was born in Dickson County, Tenn., June 24, 1822. His parents were James and Elizabeth (Kagan) Daniel. The father was born in North Carolina January 4, 1796, and died January 28, 1871. The mother was born July 7, 1802, and died in November, 1879. Our subject began teaching school at the age of eighteen years, and taught until the close of the war, when he engaged in merchandising at Danielsville until 1876. Since then he has looked after the interests of his farm. He was elected to the office of magistrate of Dickson County in 1864, which office he held until 1884, during which time he also served as chairman of the county court for several years. He was married, December 31, 1846, to Phoebe Cooksey, of Dickson County. To them have been born ten children: Tennessee D., Missouri H. (deceased), Bettie Georgia, Enola N., Emily A., Sallie A. (deceased), Cornelia R., Cora F., Jesse (deceased) and William H. Our subject is a Democrat.

J. A. Dodson, clerk of the Circuit Court of Dickson County, was born in Halifax County, Va., August 11, 1827. He was the third of a family of seven children born to the marriage of William and Catharine (Davis) Dodson, both natives of Virginia. The father was a tanner, and in 1828 came to Davidson County, Tenn., and settled near the Hermitage. The family removed to Maury County the next year and lived there one year; then they moved to Hickman County. In December, 1833, they came to Dickson County, where they remained till they died. The father was a soldier in the war of 1812. He died in 1883 and the mother in 1865. The subject of this sketch was reared mainly in Charlotte, securing a fair education and teaching school. At the age of twenty-one he was mercantile clerk for one year; then he opened a store and sold goods at Charlotte for three years. For eight years he vended merchandise at Kaworth's Landing, on the Cumberland River. He then enlisted in Company D, Forty-ninth Tennessee Volunteers, and served till the surrender. Coming from the war he resumed farming, which he continued till 1870, when he was elected to the office which he has held continuously ever since. He was married, in 1849, to Mary A. E. Laird, who died May 3, 1879. March 27, 1884, he chose and wedded Eliza C. Hopkins, and this union has blessed them with one daughter—Sarah C. Both he and his wife are members of the Cumberland Presbyterian Church. He has always been a Democrat, and is recognized as one of the prominent and public spirited citizens of Dickson County.

William Easley was born in Hickman County, Tenn., January 27, 1828. His father was born in South Carolina in 1798, and came to Tennessee in 1812, and died in 1854. The mother was born in North Carolina in 1803 and died in 1883. Our subject was married, February 29, 1854, to Susanna Sugg. They have five children: Susanna E., born February 18, 1856; John B. L., born May 29, 1858, and died June 16, 1859; Mary Jane, born November 6, 1859; William J., born December 10, 1861, and Benjamin F., born December 15, 1867. In 1863 our subject enlisted in the Confederate Army, joining the Ninth Tennessee Cavalry. At the close of the war he came home and engaged in farming, which occupation he has successfully followed up to the present time. He and wife are members of the Methodist Episcopal Church South. He is a Democrat and enjoys the esteem of his fellow-citizens.

Stephen G. Eleazer is the son of Stephen G. and Elizabeth (Bibb) Eleazer and was born at Turnbull Forge in Dickson County, Tenn., September 25, 1833. His father was a native of South Carolina and died of cholera in 1835. His mother was born in Tennessee, her grandfather being one of the earliest settlers of the State. Our subject began work for himself at the age of twenty-four years, engaging in farm work, which he continued until the breaking out of the Rebellion, when he entered the Confederate service, he being one of the first to volunteer, and went out under Col. Bailey. He was taken prisoner at Fort Donelson and confined at Camp Douglas as a prisoner of war for seventeen months. After the prisoners were exchanged at Vicksburg, Miss., and the company was reorganized he was appointed a commissary sergeant. Our subject went through the war without having been sworn into the service. On May 5, 1858, he was married to Susanna Woodard and to them were born eight children: Benjamin F., Sallie C., William M., Sleven G., George, John D., Elizabeth and Susie Ann. The wife died in 1882. Our subject is a successful farmer and a prominent man. He was elected and served as trustee of his county during 1874-75 and served as tax collector from 1876 to 1879.

Jonathan W. Elliott was born in Stewart County, Tenn., November 124, 1826. His father was born in Virginia in 1790 and died in 1866. The mother was born in North Carolina in 1805 and died in 1876. Our subject began farming at the age of twenty-one years, and continued in that business until 1866, when he engaged in general merchandising. March 20, 1880, he moved to Barton's

Creek, three miles north of Charlotte, where he now lives. He was united in marriage July 8, 1850, to Isabella M. Wall. To them was born one child, Alma W., born March 23, 1851. The wife dying December 12, 1865, our subject was married to Arabella M. Wall. This union has resulted in five children: May, born February 10, 1868, and died May 23, 1874; Charlie, born June 13, 1870; Claude, born February 16, 1872; Allen F., born February 15, 1876, and Wall, born October 6, 1877. Our subject is a member of the Masonic fraternity, Charlotte Lodge, No. 97. He and wife are members of the Methodist Episcopal Church South.

R. D. Eubank, trustee of Dickson County, is a son of John and Eliza (Crumpler) Eubank, natives of Halifax County, Va., and Dickson County, Tenn., respectively. The father came to Montgomery County, Tenn., when young and served an apprenticeship to the tailor's trade, and then opened a tailor shop at Charlotte, where he continued at his trade until a few years previous to the war, when he engaged at farming, and was identified with public affairs. He served ten years in the State Legislature. He is now living about three miles east of Charlotte, having been born October 10, 1804. Our subject was reared on a farm and remained with his parents to the age of twenty-two, when he married. He was born March 14, 1839. In 1861 he enlisted in Company D, Forty-ninth Tennessee Volunteers, and remained in the service until the spring of 1865. Since the war he has followed farming. In 1880 he was elected trustee of Dickson County, and is now the incumbent of the office. In 1860 he was married to Lucinda Corlew, who bore him four children, one son and three daughters: Leona, Catharine, Ada B. and Richard D. He was bereft of his wife September 17, 1882. She was a member of the Methodist Episcopal Church. Mr. Eubank and one child are members of the Cumberland Presbyterian Church. Politically he is a Democrat and one of the highly respected citizens of Dickson County.

Rufus Ferbee was born in Dickson County, Tenn., February 6, 1831, being the youngest of six children born to Thomas and Mrs. Ferbee. The parents were natives of Norfolk County, Va., Our subject began farming at the age of twenty years, which occupation he followed for about twenty years, and has been quite successful in his business ventures. He has served one term as sheriff of Dickson County, and has also filled the office of constable, being elected to the latter office about 1871, and served two years. December 31, 1859, he was united in marriage to Elena S. Harris, and to them have been born twelve children— seven sons and five daughters—two of whom are dead. Our subject is at present engaged in farming, and is a highly respected citizen and a man of considerable influence in his community. He is a Democrat politically.

Col. Thomas K. Grigsby, one of Dickson County's prominent citizens and clerk of the county court, was born July 31, 1823, in Madison County, Ala., being the second of a family of eight children of Samuel and Dorcas (Wyly) Grigsby. The parents lived and died in Alabama, the father's occupation being that of a farmer. When our subject was but about seventeen years old he left home and began life for himself, working about on farms for two years. At the age of nineteen he came to Waverly, Tenn., and engaged as clerk in a store. In this vocation he continued until 1848, when he married and came to Charlotte and began merchandising, in which he was very successful until 1861. He then enlisted in Company B, Forty-ninth Tennessee, as captain. He was captured at Fort Donelson and retained as prisoner nine months. Upon the reorganization of the regiment he was elected lieutenant-colonel and was promoted to the colonelcy, which he resigned on account of physical disability. Returning home he engaged at, farming for a few years. In 1870 he was elected to the office of which he is now the incumbent and has held it continuously by re-election ever since. He is extensively interested in real estate, and now owns over 3,000 acres of land. He was married in 1846 to Sarah A. Priestley, the result of this union being four children. The eldest son, James P., was a physician, and died of the yellow fever while bravely caring for those distressed at Erin in 1878. The others are Samuel W., William D. and Theodosia (the wife of D. S. Major of Cheatham County). This wife died in 1871, and Mr. Grigsby then chose and wedded, in 1874, Jane Hendrick, of Jefferson County, Tenn., by nativity. Five children have blessed this union, two of whom died in infancy, named Kelly and Mabel. The others are Thomas K., John W. and Harris. Both Mr. Grigsby and his wife are members of the Methodist Episcopal Church South. Politically he was formerly an old line Whig, casting his first vote, for Henry Clay. He is now a firm Democrat and is justly recognized as the most popular citizen of Dickson County.

William L. Grigsby, clerk and master of the Dickson County Chancery Court, was born March 25, 1854, in Dickson County. He was the youngest child born to the marriage of Thomas K. Grigsby and Sarah E. Priestley. The father's sketch appears above. William L. was reared in Charlotte and received a good early education in Tracy Academy and also attended commercial college at Nashville. His education did not stop with his schooling, he has been a close student all his major life and is a fine scholar. He was employed as deputy in county court clerk's office, of which his father was the incumbent, to the age of twenty- one years. He also read law while thus engaged. On the day of attaining his majority he made his first law speech in a suit of $10,000 and since then he has been engaged in the practice of his profession, being now recognized as the leading member of the Dickson County bar. He was

appointed to the office which he how holds in 1880, to fill an un-
expired term. In 1884 he was reappointed. He deals very extensively in real estate and now owns about 4,000 acres of land. May
26, 1874, at the age of twenty he was united in marriage to Rosa
McNeilly, a native of this county and daughter of John McNeilly, a
prominent pioneer of the county. This union has been blessed in
the birth of five children, one of whom (Annie) died in infancy.
The others are Allie, Virgil, Homer and Clide. Mr. Grigsby and his
wife are members of the Methodist Episcopal Church and Mr.
Grigsby is steward in the church. He is also a member of K. & L. of
H., K. of H. and Masonic fraternities. In the first named order he
was honored with the commission as the State delegate to the Supreme National Convention in 1885 at Chicago. Politically he is a
firm Democrat. He was delegate to the National Democratic Convention at Chicago in 1882. In this county and in this section of
the State he is thoroughly known and highly respected, and he is
one of the prominent men of the State, although he has always
declined to accept political honor.

Samuel W. Grigsby, sheriff of Dickson, is the third of Thomas
K. Grigsby's family. He was born January 26, 1852, in Charlotte,
where he was raised. He remained with his parents to the age of
seventeen and then went to Alabama, where he remained a short
time. He returned and at the age of eighteen engaged in saw-
milling on the Cumberland River in which he continued ten
months. He then went to Texas and farmed three years. He then
returned to Dickson County and has ever since carried on farming
in the county, and now owns 140 acres of land. From 1876 to 1878
he was justice of the peace in District No. 6. He was elected sheriff
of Dickson County in 1884 and is now the incumbent of the office. He was married, in 1869, to F. C. Hassell, a native of Dickson
County. Five children have been born to this union, one of whom,

Edwene, died in infancy. The others are Thomas W., Pearl P., Annie T., and James L. Himself and wife are members of the Methodist Episcopal Church South. He is a member of the Democratic party and of the F. & A. M. organization. As a citizen he is recognized as a valued member of the community.

Joe Grimes was born in Dickson County, Tenn., October 1, 1809, being the sixth of thirteen children born to the marriage of John and Margery (Carmack) Grimes. Both parents were natives of Virginia; the father was born January 2, 1775, and the mother in 1779. Our subject remained on the farm with his father until February 12, 1835, when he was married to Huldah Jane Walker. To them were born four children: Susan E., born March 16, 1836; John P., born October 10, 1842; Cornelius, born June 30, 1845, and Mary M., born February 17, 1849. The wife dying September 22, 1875, our subject was married to the widow of Gabriel Andrews. At different times Mr. Grimes served as constable, deputy sheriff and trustee of his county, serving in each office about two years. He is a member of the Free-Will Baptist Church, and is a Democrat in his political views.

John P. Grimes was born in Dickson County, Tenn., October 10, 1842, being a son of Joe and Hulda Jane (Walker) Grimes. At the age of seventeen years he enlisted in the Confederate Army in 1861 under Capt. Mallory, Company E, Eleventh Tennessee Regiment, for twelve months, and served throughout the War, receiving a severe wound in the thigh at Chickamauga, which disabled him for work a year, during which time he was confined in the hospital at Montgomery, Ala. He now resides with his father, having never married. He is about forty-four years of age, and is quite well to do in worldly goods. He is a Democrat and highly respected by his neighbors.

Dr. J. T. Henslee, one of Dickson County's most prominent citizens, was born May 5, 1838, in western Kentucky, being one of a family of children born to the marriage of Joab Henslee and Nancy Justice. The father was a native of South Carolina, was a farmer and lived and died in Kentucky, his death occurring at the age of eighty-three years in 1878. The mother was a native of North Carolina, and at the age of eighty-six years, on Christmas day, 1885, she joined the innumerable dead. The immediate subject of this sketch was reared on a farm in his native State, and secured a common school education. He remained with his parents to the age of twenty-six years, having been in the war two years, in the Seventh Kentucky Volunteers, Confederate States Army. After his service in the war he studied medicine and attended the Medical College at Nashville, and in 1870 graduated in the Vanderbilt Medical College, having practiced about three years before receiving his diploma. He then engaged in the practice of his profession very successfully in Carroll County until 1879, when he located at Dickson in the practice of medicine, and also in general merchandising, including drugs. He justly met with very great success in his profession. In 1885 he retired from active practice to take charge of his business exclusively, transacting a business of about $20,000 per year. In 1870 he was married to M. F. Lipe, of Carroll County, who bore him one son, Pitt, now fourteen years old. This wife died in 1873, and in 1879 he chose and wedded D. M. Pickier, also of Carroll County. One daughter, Floy, has blessed this union. Mrs. Henslee is a member of the Missionary Baptist Church. Dr. Henslee is a member of the F. & A. M., K. of H. and K. & L. of H. orders. Politically he is a firm Democrat, and is widely known as an energetic and enterprising citizen.

Elbert J. Hicks was born in Dickson County, Tenn., May 6, 1821. His parents were James and Mary (Marlow) Hicks, the father being born in Virginia in 1781. The mother was born in North Carolina. Our subject was united in marriage, January 23, 1845, to Mariah C. Houston, who was born in Dickson County, Tenn., February 21, 1827. The result of this union has been eleven children: Martha E., born October 25, 1845, and died August 17, 1863; Mary J., born March 20, 1847; Sallie T., born January 15, 1849; James S., born February 28, 1851; John F., born April 18, 1853; Robert H., born May 20, 1856; Laura D., born November 5, 1858; Lula H., born August 29, 1861; Martha E., born January 30, 1864; Hester L., born October 7, 1866, and Faustina H. born April 27, 1872. Our subject is now justice of the peace of this district and chairman of the county court. He has served as magistrate for ten years. He is a member of the Cumberland Presbyterian Church, and his wife belongs to the Methodist Episcopal Church South. Politically he is a Democrat.

James C. Hunt was born at Clarksville, Montgomery Co., Tenn., July 28, 1839. His parents were Solomon and Ann R. (Hillyard) Hunt. The father was a native of North Carolina, and came to Tennessee about 1835. He was a prominent farmer and died in 1841. The mother was a native of Virginia. At the age of eighteen our subject was engaged as clerk at Williamsville for W. D. Balthrop, merchant, and remained with him two years, when he was married, November 17, 1859, to Serenia P. Slaydon. This union has resulted in nine children: William T., born July 23, 1860; Theodosia, born in 1862; Robert B., born in 1864, and died in his childhood; Solomon E., born February 5, 1867; Albert P., born August 20, 1869; John Franklin, born in 1871; James Morris, born in 1873; Noel Clarence, born in 1875, and Hartwell Slaydon, born in 1877. Our subject entered the Confederate Army, under

Gen. Forrest, in 1861, in Company C, Tenth Tennessee Cavalry, and served throughout the war without receiving a single wound. He and wife are members of the Methodist Episcopal Church South. He is a member of the Masonic fraternity, belonging to Yellow Creek Lodge, No. 319, and is a Democrat. He is a man of much influence in his community, and has accumulated a nice sum of money.

James Washington Hunter, a resident of the Seventh District of Dickson County, Tenn., first saw the light of day March 2, 1836. He is the eldest of six children of Burrell and Hixey R. (Simms) Hunter, both born in Dickson County. Our subject received a common school education, after which he farmed with his father and worked to some extent at the carpenter's trade. He was married, December 6, 1863, to Miss Martha Ann Pinson, who was resident of Dickson County, and was born May 10, 1845. Their union was blessed by the birth of six children—three of whom are now living: William Benjamin, Eva and Erwin B. Our subject and his wife are worthy members of the Methodist Episcopal Church South, and in politics Mr. Hunter favors the principles of the Democratic party. His present property consists of 100 acres of good and well cultivated land on the Harpeth and Charlotte road. He also owns a blacksmith shop on the same property. He has been engaged in different occupations and is considered a good citizen.

James G. Jackson was born in Dickson County, Tenn., February 12, 1820, and was the son of Epps and Elizabeth (Boss) Jackson. The father was born in Virginia in 1796 and died in 1851. The mother was born in Dickson County, Tenn., and lived there until her death. Our subject was engaged as business manager at the Wayne County Iron Works when but twenty-one years old, which position he held for about five years. In 1848 his father founded the Webster Furnace in Montgomery County, of which James G. was given the management until 1850, when his father completed the furnace in Humphreys County called Hurricane Forge, and he took charge of that. He afterward came to Barton's Creek, three miles north of Charlotte, where he engaged in farming, at which occupation he is still employed. In October, 1844, he was married to Susan Eleazor. They have no children. He is a man of good standing in his community.

W. J. Mathis, a prominent merchant and proprietor of a livery stable, was born April 29, 1837, in Charlotte, Tenn., being the eldest of five children born to the marriage of Wilson J. Mathis and Louisa Roberts. The father was born in 1808 in Montgomery County. He was a cabinet-maker and farmer. He is now living near Charlotte, one of the prominent old citizens of the county, having been sheriff of the county a number of terms, and in the State Legislature two terms. The mother was a native of Dickson County and died when our subject was quite young. The subject of this sketch was reared with his parents in Charlotte to the age of eighteen, when he engaged as clerk at Ashland Furnace for two years.

He then went to Palmyra and clerked in a store for several years, and after a trip to Texas joined Company C, Eleventh Tennessee Volunteers, as first lieutenant, and upon the reorganization of the company was made adjutant of the Eleventh Regiment. He was wounded by a gun-shot in the wrist. Returning from the army he engaged as clerk for a number of years. Then he married and farmed one and a half years. In 1870 he was made deputy clerk of the county court. He then moved to Hill County, Tex., and farmed one year; thence to Waco, Tex., where he followed auctioneering.

From there he returned to Dickson County, Tenn., and in a short time opened, on a very limited scale, a family grocery store. He now carries a complete line of general merchandise and manages a first-class livery. He was married, September 10, 1868, to Sarah E. Larkins. He was reared in the air of Democracy, and is now a firm member of that party. As a citizen he is well respected.

Anthony A. Matthews, a native of Dickson County, Tenn., and a resident of Bellsburg, was born December 6, 1848, and is the eldest of five children of Buckner W. and Sarah C. (Weakley) Matthews, natives of Virginia and Tennessee, respectively. Our subject received a common school education, and when twenty-four years of age left home and engaged in selling fruit trees for two years. He then returned home and followed farming two years. He at that time went to Cumberland Furnace, and was over-seer of the Furnace farm for one year. He then clerked four years in the Furnace store, and next engaged in the merchandise business with C. J. Phillips two years near Cumberland Furnace. He then sold out to his partner and purchased a stock of goods of J. P. Eleazor, and has succeeded quite well financially. November 10, 1880, he wedded Alice V. Hooper, a resident of Cheatham County. Our subject and his wife are members of the Episcopal Church. Mr. Matthews is a Mason, and has been constable two years and postmaster at Bellsburg one year. He is a Democrat.

J. D. Martin was born in Dickson County, Tenn., July 13, 1835. His father was born in Virginia in 1810, and his mother in this State in 1812. The father served as sheriff of Dickson County for a number of years before the war. Our subject engaged in farming until the war, when he enlisted in Company E, Tenth Tennessee Cavalry, and served throughout the war, receiving only a flesh wound. On his return from the war he continued his farming, which occupation he has successfully followed up to the present. He was married April 8, 1858, to Amanda J. England, of this county. Four children have been born to them: Eunice A., Edward F., Hester L. and John E. His wife was a member of the Methodist Episcopal Church South, and died May 18, 1868. Our subject was again married in December, 1868, to Matilda M. England. The result of this union is five children: Cora D., William M., Ludova J., Samuel J. Tilden, and Emily M. Our subject is a Democrat and a man of good standing in the community. He has been very successful and is considered, probably, one of the most substantial men of his district.

William B. McFarland was born in Greenville, Mercer Co., Penn., October 11, 1826, being the son of Samuel and Lutitia (Beem) McFarland. The parents were natives of Mercer County, Penn., the father being born October, 1799, and the mother about 1804, the latter dying in September, 1880. Our subject came to Tennessee in June, 1867, and bought the farm on which he now resides, which is situated one-half mile north of Dickson. December 27, 1849, he was married to Elizabeth Biddle, also a native of Pennsylvania. This union has resulted in five children: Robert B.; Samuel O., died November 3, 1874; John P.; Seth P., died October 2, 1882, and Elizabeth L. His wife died September 11, 1880, a faithful member of the Methodist Episcopal Church. Our subject is a man of considerable influence in his community. In politics he is a believer in and an advocate of the principles of Republicanism.

Rev. W. G. McMillan, a prominent citizen of Charlotte, was born September 14, 1846, in what is now Houston County, being the second of a family of twelve children of Daniel G. and Sallie Anne (Nichols) McMillan, Natives of Houston County. He was reared on a farm, and secured a limited, early education, which he has much improved in his leisure hours. He has taught school about seventeen years. He is also a good surveyor, and learned the art under W. H. Fessey, of Montgomery County. He was elected county surveyor of Houston County in 1875, and held the position till 1877. He then removed to Dickson County and followed teaching till 1885, having been superintendent of instruction of the county from 1878 to 1884. In July, 1885, he was elected county surveyor of Dickson County, in the duties of which he is now employed. He is also a farmer by occupation, and owns 343 acres of land, 100 acres of which is bottom land and very valuable. He was married, December 27, 1876, to Susie Hutton, a native of Dickson County, the result of this union being four children: Anna, Maggie B., Fannie E. and Nora L. Himself and wife are members of the Methodist Episcopal Church South, and he is a minister in that church. He is a worthy and enterprising citizen of the county and bears the esteem of his fellow-beings.

Augustus E. C. Miller was born in Gotha, Germany, December 8, 1825, being the son of John C. and Elizabeth Miller, both of whom were natives of Germany. In 1837 John C. immigrated to Pennsylvania, in which State he lived until his death. Elizabeth was born in 1798, and died November, 1878, in Dickson County. Our subject was the eldest child, his brother, Herman, being born in 1827, and his sister, Louisa, in 1830. At the age of twenty-five years our subject began teaming at the Pennsylvania Canal, at which he worked for about three years, when he began piloting on the above canal. Afterward he was captain of the "J. W. Igo," and subsequently owned and ran several boats in the same stream. In 1853 he sold his boats and engaged in farming in Pennsylvania, and in 1869 he came to Dickson County, Tenn., where he now lives. In 1851 he was married to Elizabeth J. Goan, of Pennsylvania, and to this union were born fifteen children, ten of whom are yet living. His wife dying he was married, June 10, 1883, to Laura

E. Mitchell, and he and his wife are members of the Methodist Episcopal Church South. Our subject is a man of wealth, having accumulated about $15,000 by his own exertions. He has in his possession a pair of shoes which he wore at the age of one year, and has also an old German hymn-book which has been in the family for over 100 years. He was a man of considerable influence in Pennsylvania, and although receiving but three weeks' education in the English language is a very good English scholar. He takes much interest in church affairs, and has been in sight of the place where Martin Luther translated the Bible.

Pasivent S. Miller was born in Pennsylvania January 2, 1859, being the son of A. E. C. and Elizabeth (Goan) Miller. He is of German descent, and February 9, 1880, was united in marriage to Elizabeth E. Riser, who was also a native of Pennsylvania. To them one child was born, Cassius H., born October 26, 1881, and died March 3, 1883. Our subject has been engaged in farming interests all his life. Politically he is a Democrat and a man of good standing in his community.

John B. Monroe was born in North Carolina February 10, 1820, being the son of Johnson and Sallie (Hanks) Monroe. The father, with our subject, came to Tennessee in 1844, the mother having died when our subject was but three years old. The father died in Christian County, Ky., in 1858. Our subject was married March 1, 1849, to Nancy Ann Luttrel. The union has resulted in eleven children: Sarah E., born November 27, 1849 (deceased); Leegran, born May 25, 1851; Andrew J., born November 1, 1853; Rosa I., born March 5, 1856 (deceased); John W., born October 31, 1858; Susie W., born July 26, 1861; Mary C., born March 26, 1864; Robert J., born July 16, 1866 (deceased); Nancy A., born December 27, 1868; Thomas W., born December 21, 1871, and Elv-

ira M., born October 31, 1877. Our subject has been an agricultur-
ist all his life. In November, 1861, he entered the civil war, under
T. Grigsby, at Charlotte, where he served for eighteen months,
being taken prisoner at Fort Donelson. He is a member of the
Methodist Episcopal Church South. Politically he is a Democrat.
His wife is a member of the Free-Will Baptist Church.

James Martin Moody was born in Dickson County, Tenn.,
June 8, 1845. He is the son of William and Charity E. (Gardner)
Moody. The father was born in Cheatham County, now Robertson, February 14, 1818, and was a graduate of the Philadelphia
Medical College, and practiced his profession in Dickson County
for over forty years, and died September 12, 1885. The mother
was born in Sumner County, Tenn., November 25, 1826, and is
still living, making her home with her son, Oscar N., at Gillem,
Tenn. Our subject entered the Confederate Army at the age of
seventeen, joining the Tenth Tennessee Calvary in Company E.,
and participated in a number of engagements. Ill health compelled
him to leave the army in 1864, and returning home he entered his
father's store at Gillem and remained there about three years,
when he went to Texas and engaged at saw-milling. Two years
later he returned to Tennessee. He was married to Maggie Blanks,
of Dickson County, December 22, 1869, and to them have been
born seven children: Florence, Claudie Lee, William Augustus,
Elma, Alexander, Eugenia, Gulnah, Benjamin Franklin and Walker Edwards. After his marriage he engaged in farming, which he
has successfully followed up to the present time. He was elected
magistrate of the First District in 1874, and served three years
when he resigned. At present he is acting as agent of the Tennessee & Chicago Land Company. He and wife are members of the
Methodist Episcopal Church South. He is a Democrat.

Dr. Oscar Noel Moody is a practicing physician of Tennessee City, being the son of William and Charity E. (Gardner) Moody. The father was born February 14, 1818, in Cheatham County, Tenn., and was a physician; he died September 12, 1885. The mother was born in Sumner County, Tenn., November 25, 1826. Our subject graduated March, 1882, at University of Nashville and Vanderbilt University at Nashville; since then he has been a successful practitioner. He is unmarried and living with his mother, who is now sixty years of age. His educational advantages were very good, having been educated at Montgomery Bell's College. Politically he is a Democrat, and as a man and citizen is much esteemed.

Thomas C. Morris, a prominent attorney of Charlotte, was born September 27, 1833, in Charlotte, being the third of a family of six children of James K. and Eliza (McNeilly) Morris, natives of Tennessee. The father was a blacksmith and died in 1860 in Christian County, Ky., where he had lived a number of years. The mother passed from the living in 1844. The subject of this sketch was reared on a farm in Humphreys County to the age of seventeen, when, in 1850, he came to Charlotte and began reading law, while engaged as deputy clerk in the county court. In 1854 he began the practice of law, and has ever since been a member of the Dickson County bar. In 1859 he was elected by the county court as its clerk, and in 1860 was re-elected by the people and held the office until the close of the war. Since that time he has been engaged in the practice of his profession and farming, now owning over 200 acres of land. He was a member of the State Constitutional Convention in 1870. Politically he is a firm Democrat. He was married, November 26, 1858, to Martha E. Rye, who lived to be the mother of five children, one of whom, Margaret G., died at two years of age. The others are Mary M., Robert J., Lizzie C. and

James R. His wife died September 27, 1878, and in September, 1880, he was married to Anne G. Nesbitt, his present wife, who, with Mr. Morris, is a member of the Methodist Episcopal Church. Mr. Morris is a member of the K. & L. of H., K. of H. and F. & A. M. fraternities. He is an honorable and upright citizen of the community, and an able lawyer in Dickson County.

Col. George H. Morton, a highly respected and esteemed citizen of White Bluff, Tenn., was born October 10, 1836, in Haddington, Scotland, being the youngest of eleven children of Thomas D. and Marguerite (Donrad) Morton. The father was a native of Scotland and the mother was of French descent. Col. Morton received a liberal education in his native land, and at the age of fifteen came to the United States and worked at the carpenter's trade and at merchandising until the breaking out of the late war, when he enlisted under Capt. McNairy of the First Battalion Tennessee Cavalry, Confederate States Army. By his faithful and efficient service he was raised from a private to the rank of lieutenant-colonel. He was wounded six times, but at present suffers but little from the effects. May 1, 1866, he was married to Miss Dora Donelson, and to them were born seven children: George H., Thomas D., Turner H., James T., William Lee, Norman H. and Dora. Col. Morton is a member of the F. & A. M., I. O. O. F. and K. of H. He is at present engaged in the general merchandise business at White Bluff and carries a stock valued from $3,000 to $4,000. He was burned out in 1882, but with the exception of that has been quite fortunate in his business transactions.

Thomas J. Murrell was born in Dickson County, Tenn., January 11, 1825, the son of Thomas and Ella (Coen) Murrell, both of whom were natives of East Tennessee. The father was trustee of Dickson County for seventeen years. Our subject was first engaged in farming, which occupation he followed for twelve years, when he engaged in merchandising at Dickson, Tenn. He was married, December 28, 1845, to Mary Eliza Austin, who was also born in Tennessee. Their marriage has been blessed by ten children: Elenora, Mary Elizabeth (deceased), Missouri Alice, Thomas Franklin (deceased), James Samuel, Mary Franklin, George B. (deceased), William M., Lucinda E. (deceased) and Nannie Beulah. Our subject is a successful merchant and an influential citizen.

William M. Murrell was born in Dickson County, Tenn., October 3, 1862, being one of ten children born to Thomas J. and Mary Eliza (Austin) Murrell. Our subject was raised on the farm until his fifteenth year, at which time he entered school at Dickson, taking a five years' course. After leaving school he returned to the farm and remained for two years. He then engaged in merchandising at Dickson, which business he successfully follows. He was married, October 18, 1885, to Mattie H. Andrews, who was born in Hickman County, Tenn. Politically, he is a Democrat.

Kendrick Myatt was born May 22, 1822, in Tennessee, the fifth of nine children. Our subject began work on the farm for himself at the age of twenty years, continuing at that avocation for about thirty years, during which time he was very successful. He then engaged in the saw and grist-mill business and carding machine, continuing at that for about five years. He has been postmaster at Burns' Station for twelve years, and was railroad agent about eight years of that time. He engaged in merchandising for a number of years and was burned out in 1879. In January, 1840, he was married to Cynthia Laftis, and to them were born seven children. His wife dying he was married to Jane Boss, and by her had one child, and, being again left a widower, he married Mary Jane Lambert, and by her has five children. The educational advantages of our subject were limited, yet he has been a very successful man

throughout life, and is a man of reliability and influence. Politically, he is a Democrat.

Allston Myatt, a prominent merchant of Dickson, was born
January 24, 1824, in Dickson County, Tenn., being the sixth of ten
children born to the union of Kendrick and Elizabeth (Harmon)
Myatt, both natives of North Carolina. In 1818 the father came to
Dickson County where he followed farming until 1860, the year of
his death. The mother died in August, 1885, at the age of ninety-
four years. Our subject was reared with his parents on a farm to
the age of twenty-one, when he went to Kentucky where he
taught school two years. He then returned, married and began
farming. He was county surveyor for eighteen years. In 1868 he
opened a general merchandise establishment in Dickson and continued one year. He was then appointed by the governor as commissioner of registration and served in that capacity till the repeal
of the act supporting the office. In 1872 he resumed his business
and has continued it successfully, although with some trying ad-
versities. He now owns about 2,000 acres of land. He was married,
December 25, 1847, to Mary Ann Sugg, the result of this union
being nine children, three of whom are now living: Kendrick H.,
James A. and Benjamin F. This wife died in 1869 and he then
chose and wedded, December 25, 1870, Mrs. S. M. Fox. Four children bless this union: Samuel A. and Charlie A. (twins), Theodore
L. and Mary C. Mr. Myatt and wife are members of the Methodist
Episcopal Church South. He is a member of the F. & A. M. He was
a Whig before the war and is a Democrat since. He is one of the
enterprising citizens of Dickson.

William T. Nesbitt was born October 25, 1845, and is the son
of Andrew F. and Nancy (Dilleha) Nesbitt. The parents were born
in Tennessee, the father in 1820. He was a first lieutenant in the

Confederate Army, and was killed at Brentwood while leading Capt. Minor's company. At the age of eighteen years our subject entered the Confederate Army, joining Company E, Tenth Tennessee Cavalry. He returned home after the surrender and engaged in school teaching for eight years. In 1874 he joined the Tennessee Conference, in which he remained about eleven years when he was located. December 26, 1876, he was married to Mrs. Cornelia White, nee Moore. To them four children have been born: Robert Moore White, Julia Edna Parthenia, Wilbur Foster, and Edgar Jones. Our subject is a Democrat.

Jerry Nesbitt was born in Dickson County, Tenn., June 14, 1848, and is the son of Andrew F. and Nancy (Dilleha) Nesbitt. The father was justice of the peace for several years. His death occurred March 26, 1863 (see W. T. Nesbitt for sketch of father). The mother was born in Dickson County in 1824, and died in 1866. Our subject was but fifteen years old at the time of his father's death, and has since then been at work for himself, being a farmer by occupation. February 24, 1875, he was married to Minerva J. Dickson, who was born in Houston County March 29, 1856. They have three children: Andrew J., Lillie Bell and Clarence Y. The wife is a member of the Cumberland Presbyterian Church. Politically our subject is a Democrat.

William J. A. Nesbitt was born in Dickson County, Tenn., February 14, 1840, being the eldest of eleven children. He entered the Confederate Army as a volunteer in May, 1861, joining Company C, Eleventh Tennessee Infantry. He was discharged October 18, 1861, on account of his health. The following August he joined Company E, Eleventh Tennessee Cavalry. He was captured December 20, 1863, and imprisoned at Rock Island, where he remained until February 28, 1865. Afterward he volunteered in the

United States Army in Company G, Third United States Regiment, and served in Kansas and Colorado, and was mustered out at Fort Leavenworth, Kas., and returned home December 28, 1865. On his return he engaged in farming on Yellow Creek, where he has since continued at that occupation. He was married, August 31, 1868, to Sally Sligh. To them were born three children: Zudie Ellis, Reuel E. and Martha Susan (died April 22, 1884). In politics he is a Democrat.

Rev. George W. Nichols was born in Dickson County, Tenn., January 1, 1841, son of Nicholas H. and Eliza (Prather) Nichols. The father was born in Kentucky September 23, 1785, and came to Tennessee in 1831, locating at Lafayette Furnace, being manager of the same. Remaining there for twenty years, he moved to Bear Creek, Dickson County, where he lived until his death, which occurred in 1874. The mother was born in Maryland in 1793. Our subject engaged in school teaching for several years, after which he engaged in farming. In 1874 he was licensed to preach by the Yellow Creek Quarterly Conference, and in 1882 he was ordained by the Tennessee Annual Conference. In the year 1885 he was transferred from the Methodist Episcopal Church South to the Cumberland Presbyterian Church. Since that time he has been regularly engaged in the ministry as a member of the Charlotte Presbytery. He was married, November 13, 1862, to Arrena S. Adkins. This union has been blessed with seven children: Beulah, Agnes (deceased), L. Ramah, Floudie V., Bovin G., Lester P. and Vida V. Our subject is a Democrat.

Barton W. S. Nicks was born in Hickman County, Tenn., and is the son of Absalom D. and Hester (Perry) Nicks. Absalom was born in North Carolina March 6, 1794, and came to Hickman County in 1800, engaging in farming and transporting salt to Salem, Ill. He moved to Arkansas in the fall of 1847 and died in 1848. Hester was born in South Carolina October 8, 1788, and died at Williamsport, Maury Co., Tenn., July, 1858. Our subject remained with his parents until twenty-two years of age, and then began manufacturing poplar shingles, and after a year's time engaged in transporting dry goods, groceries, cotton, etc., to Columbia and Williamsport. He then came to Montgomery County and entered the employ of Robert Baxter at the furnaces and forges. After working there four years he returned to Williamsport in 1850 and again engaged in teaming and farming. From there he went to Laurel Furnace, in Dickson County, and hauled pig-iron to Nashville for about three years. He was coal manager at Cumberland Furnace for a number of years. At present he is engaged in farming and stock raising three miles below the furnace. Our subject was married to America Agnes McGraw, who was born October 6, 1831, and to them have been born ten children: Mary R., born November 8, 1848; Martha E., born May 20, 1851; Henry Clay, born March 6, 1854; Newton C., born March 7, 1856, and died October 13, 1875; James Franklin, born January 22, 1858; Eudora Ann, born November 22, 1859; Ellenora W., born December 24, 1861, and died May 4, 1864; Barton W. S., Jr., born June 25, 1863; Florence A., born September 28, 1865, and Stephen U., born December 10, 1867, and died January 7, 1769. Mr. Nicks is a self-made man, and is worth about $8,000.

James F. Nicks was born at Cumberland Furnace, Dickson Co., Tenn., January 22, 1858, the fifth of ten children. December 24, 1879, he was married to Eliza H. Bartee, of Dickson County, and to them have been born three children: Jasper Newton, born January 24, 1881, and died January 11, 1885; Addie Lee, born June 6, 1883; Eula Agnes, born December 3, 1885. Our subject is a farmer by occupation, having followed that vocation since his nineteenth year. His educational advantages were limited, but he has made the most of his opportunities, and is a man highly esteemed by his neighbors. He is a member of the Democratic party, and he and wife are members of the Christian Church.

William J. Norris was born in Dickson County, Tenn., January 27, 1844. His parents were William W. and Elizabeth (Balthrop) Norris, both of whom were natives of Tennessee. The father was born January 29, 1810; the mother March 24, 1815, and died December 2,1858. Our subject enlisted in the Confederate Army in 1862, joining the Tenth Tennessee Cavalry. Remaining in the army but eighteen months he returned home and entered school, after which he taught for several months. After engaging in several other occupations he entered as partner with T. Rogers in the mill and merchandise business at Cave Mills, at which he continued for ten years, when he sold his interest and bought the farm that he now lives on, two miles north of Cave Mills on Yellow Creek. While at the above named place he was postmaster. He was married, October 15, 1865, to Dollie Ann Thompson. She was born in Dickson County, March 4, 1847. To this union eight children have been born: William J., Lillie Ann, Donie Alice, Minnie, Daisy, Milton, Mary and Jennie, of whom Milton and Mary are dead. Our subject has a fair education. He is a Democrat.

A. E. Pardue was born near Cheap Hill, Cheatham Co., Tenn., and is the youngest of six children born to the marriage of Oliver Pardue and Erilla Reeves, who were born in North Carolina and Tennessee, respectively. Our subject received but limited school advantages, and is now a self-educated man. His mother died when he was quite small, and the family was separated, he going to Illinois to live with an uncle. He returned to Tennessee after a period of five years, and then went to the blue-grass State, where he lived with his brother for two years. He then returned to Tennessee and enlisted in the Second Tennessee Regiment, Confederate States Army, under Col. Bates and Capt. Chaney, and served four years, participating in the battles of Bull Run, Shiloh, Franklin, Perryville, Chickamauga, Atlanta, Missionary Ridge, Nashville and many skirmishes. He was wounded at the latter battle. December 28, 1871, he wedded Miss Bettie Edwards, a native of Dickson County. He and wife are members of the Cumberland Presbyterian and Methodist Episcopal Churches, respectively. Since the war Mr. Pardue has resided on the homestead place, the plantation containing over 1,200 acres of valuable land, all of which he has earned himself. He is a stanch Democrat and a highly respected citizen of the county, and in connection with his farming is a forwarding and commission merchant.

Cave Johnson Phillips was born April 28, 1842, being the third child of nine children born to Preston D. and Amanda (Appleton) Phillips. The father is still living, at the age of seventy-seven, with our subject. The mother died in Davidson County about the year 1857. January 18, 1871, our subject was united in marriage to Jane W. Matthews, who was born July 25, 1851. The results of this union are seven children: Rufus S., born October 13, 1871; Dottie E., born September 11, 1873; Anthony J., born January 12, 1876; Willie F., born September 21, 1878; Almedia A., born November 1, 1880 (deceased); Judie Ray, born April 6, 1882, and William L., born February 22, 1885. Our subject began business for himself at the age of twenty-nine. He first engaged in farming, where he now lives, in Dickson County, and afterward engaged in general merchandising. He has been very successful in business, having accumulated about $6,000 since 1871. He and wife are members of the Christian Church. Politically he is a Democrat and is highly respected.

Elridge Newson Phipps was born in Nashville, Tenn., April 4, 1831, and is one of twelve children born to Elridge W. and Sina (Castleman) Phipps. The father was born in 1801, and died in September, 1863. The mother was born about 1801, and died in August, 1846. Our subject engaged in farming for himself at the age of eighteen years, and continued at that occupation for eleven years. He then engaged in distilling for eight years, after which he began milling and general merchandising, which business he still follows at Shady Grove Mills, Dickson Co., Tenn. August 17, 1851, he was united in marriage to Cynthia H. Matlock, who was born July 25, 1824. She was the daughter of James and Sallie (Leesh) Matlock. Mr. and Mrs. Phipps are the parents of two daughters: Milbery, born June 6, 1852, and Mary J., born November 21, 1855; both of them are now married. Our subject is a self-made man, and has considerable influence in his community, and is worth at the present time about $13,000, all made by his own exertions. He is a Republican.

Daniel Rice was born in Strasbourg City, France, October 12, 1838. His parents dying during his infancy Daniel immigrated to the United States at the age of nineteen years, landing at New Orleans in 1851. After three years spent in horse trading he began merchandising, and continued at that business for two or three years, when he was taken sick with the yellow fever. Upon his recovery he went to Philadelphia, Penn., where he engaged for six months in the saloon business, after which he went to Wilmington, Del., where for several months he was engaged in superintending a concert. From there he came to Tennessee, locating at Charlotte, and began business as a traveling merchant in Dickson and Humphreys Counties. Our subject entered the Confederate Army in 1861, joining the Fourth Tennessee Regiment, and afterward traded places with a soldier in the Eleventh Tennessee, giving the soldier a quarter of beef to make the exchange. He was a musician for a while, and afterward commissary sergeant. He was taken prisoner at Mission Ridge November 29, 1863. May 18, 1865, he was released from prison and returned to Charlotte, where he again engaged for a few months in merchandising, when he moved his business to Johnsonville, Tenn. While at the latter place he was seriously wounded by Tom Warrin, who was intoxicated, the ball passing entirely through his body. After spending twelve months in Johnsonville he returned to Charlotte and again entered business. His marriage with Blanch A. H. Long occurred April 26, 1868. She was born in Humphreys County November 11, 1849. After his marriage he moved to Tennessee and entered business. Six children have been born to them; those living are as follows: Sophia W., born July 7, 1872; Emily Lenora, born September 29, 1876, and Katie Elizabeth, born May 8, 1884. Our subject is a Democrat and is postmaster of his town.

John Rickert, proprietor of the Dickson Trade Palace, came to Dickson County in 1867 and began farming, which he still continues. In 1871 he opened his general merchandise trade, in which he has met with success ever since. He owns about 400 acres of land adjoining Dickson, and a part of the town was laid out on his land. He was born in Pennsylvania in 1818, being the youngest of a family of nine children of Peter and Sophronia (Roth) Rickert, also natives of Pennsylvania. The parents lived and died in their native State, the father's death occurring in 1871 and the mother's in about 1865. The father was a farmer. The subject of this sketch was reared on a farm and had limited educational advantages. He married at the age of twenty-four, and followed farming in Pennsylvania till moving to Dickson County, in 1867. His marriage was in 1842 to Eliza J. Policy, of Pennsylvania. Nine children have been born to this union, viz.: Henry A., who was killed in the war; Herschel E., who died in Andersonville prison; Adolphus S., William E., John F., Maggie S. (deceased), Abner G., Elmer E. and Edwin E. Politically Mr. Rickert is a Republican, and he is one of the respected citizens of Dickson County.

Wiley M. Russell was born in Dickson County, Tenn., March 20, 1830, being the son of Lemuel S. and Nancy (Myatt) Russell. The father was born in Virginia, and came to Tennessee when quite small. The mother was a native of South Carolina. Our subject engaged in farming at the age of twenty-one years, and continued at that occupation for twelve years. He then engaged in distilling for about three years, after which time he worked some at the mechanic's trade, and then returned to his former occupation—farming—at which he is now engaged. He was married, December 4, 1850, to Serena P. Frasier. The result of this union is six children: Mary A., John D., Lauson H., James L., Silvesta and Sarah J. His wife dying in 1866 he was again married, December 15, 1866, to Sarah M. Sugg. They have six children: John, James, Lula W., Nellie R., Alford R. and Florence. Our subject was in the Confederate Army, being a member of the Forty-ninth Tennessee Regiment. In 1863 he returned home, having been discharged on account of his age. Upon his return home he was elected magistrate of Dickson County. He also served one term as constable. He is a Democrat.

Dr. John D. Slayden was born in Dickson County, Tenn., June 16, 1843, a son of Hartwell and Jane (May) Slayden. The father was born in Virginia and came to this State at a very early age. He was engaged in the mercantile business, also in farming, and was considered a very successful man. His death occurred in the spring of 1845. The mother is a native of Tennessee, and is now living with her second husband, Rev. J. J. Piskett, in Dickson County. Our subject began work for himself at the age of seventeen, and after engaging in several different occupations, among which were superintending a cotton farm in Arkansas, and at the same time learning civil engineering; began the study of medicine and continued the same for about three months, when he enlisted in the Confederate Army, joining Company C, Eleventh Tennessee Regiment. During the war he was severely wounded in the wrist. On his return he again took up the study of medicine and entered the medical college at Nashville. After having taken one course there he studied for a year under a preceptor, when he entered the Jefferson Medical College at Philadelphia, where he graduated in March, 1869. After returning home he began practicing as partner with Dr. Daniels, on Yellow Creek, but only remained with him a short time. He then came to Cumberland Furnace, Dickson County, where he now has a lucrative practice. In the winter of 1874 and 1875 he attended the hospital course in the University of New Orleans, La. September 27, 1881, he was married to Augustine M. Russell, who was born May 17, 1862. They have one child, Adella, born July 19, 1882. Our subject is a member of the Masonic fraternity. He and wife are members of the Episcopal Church. Politically he is a Democrat.

James B. Smith was born in Dickson County, Tenn., December 19, 1861, the son of John B. and Alphasarah (Von Schmittou) Smith. The father was born in Dickson County, Tenn., in 1833, and was of Irish descent. The mother was of Dutch descent, but was born in Dickson County, Tenn., in 1835. Our subject began farming at the age of twenty years, and continuing at that business until 1883, when he entered the store of James B. Stakes, at Beef range, as salesman, where he remained until December, 1884, at which time he entered business for himself at the above place.

September 3, 1882, he was united in marriage to Emma Stakes, who was born September 11, 1863. Two children have been born to them: Mattie Leona, born November 20, 1888 (deceased); Perry Barnett, born June 2, 1885. The wife is a member of the Christian Church. He is a Democrat, and is doing a good business.

John M. Speight was born at White Bluff, Dickson County, Tenn., January 7, 1856, the son of James Speight. His mother and father were both born in Dickson County, and are alive at present, living at the old homestead. At the age of seventeen our subject went to live with his uncle Benjamin McCaslin, in order to become a mechanic, and remained with him until 1876, at which time he engaged in railroading and continuing at that business for about a year, when he returned to his uncle and resumed work at his trade. Remaining two years he went to Fulton County, Ky., and worked at his trade for about eighteen months when he again returned to his uncle. He finally bought his uncle's business and ran the same until December, 1884, when he removed to Cumberland Furnace and engaged in merchandising, at which place he now resides. He was married April 30, 1882, to Eudora A. Micks. He and wife are members of the Christian Church. He is a Democrat, a self-made man, and stands high in his community.

James E. Spicer, a prominent young merchant of Dickson, was born September 10, 1858, in Humphreys County, being the second of a family of five children of Charles and Eliza E. (Long) Spicer, natives of Humphreys County. The father was a farmer and died in 1861. The mother died about 1872. James E. was reared on a farm and had limited early educational advantages. He remained with his mother to the age of nine years when he went to live with a farmer with whom he remained two years. Then he engaged as clerk in a store for about five years. In 1876 he came to

Dickson and engaged as clerk till 1882. He then opened a store with Henry E. Pickett, and continued with him for three years. In 1884 he started on his own hook his present business, in which he has been very successful. He was married, March 13, 1883, to Ida B. Williams, a native of Dickson County. One daughter, Effie L., has blessed this union. Mr. Spicer and wife are members of the Methodist Episcopal Church South. He is a member of the Good Templar organization. Politically he is a firm Democrat and is recognized as a prominent and enterprising business man and a valuable citizen.

Robert B. Stone, general manager of Cumberland Furnace, Dickson County, Tenn., was born at the furnace on September 16, 1837. His father was Hardiman Stone, who was also born in Dickson County on December 8, 1805, and died February 26, 1880. At the age of fifteen years our subject purchased his freedom from his father, paying for the same $500, and went to Texas, where he engaged in the manufactory of charcoal for two years. He then returned to the furnace where he has secured a position as manager. He was married, January 23, 1864, to Sarah M. Jackson. To this union have been born five children: Maggie V., born June 26, 1869; Epps H., born November 16, 1870; Ida F., born April 16, 1872; Effie S., born December 6, 1875, and Robert J., born March 15, 1878. Our subject's wife died March 23, 1881, and on January 15, 1885, he was married to Kate Richardson. Robert B. enlisted in the Confederate Army in 1861, being a member of the Fiftieth Tennessee Regiment. His wife is a member of the Methodist Episcopal Church, while he is an Episcopalian. He is a Democrat and a man of much influence in the county.

Mrs. J. J. Wyatt was born in Dickson County, Tenn., August 16, 1834, the daughter of Solomon and Jerusha (Darwin) Petty.

The father was born in South Carolina in 1784, and died in Dickson County in 1860. The mother was born in 1794, and died in 1873. They immigrated to Dickson County, Tenn., in 1811, where they lived until their deaths. Our subject's great-grandfather was a captain in the Revolutionary war for seven years under Gen. Green. November 16, 1854, our subject was married to William Wyatt, of Jackson County, Tenn. This union has been blessed with eight children: Eugene, Alice, Walter, James, Fanny D. (deceased), Sallie, Laura and Fredrick. Her husband is engaged as engineer for the Tennesse Manufacturing Company, at Nashville, which position he has held for fourteen years. She is a woman of fine executive ability and manages the farm in person. She and husband are members of the Christian Church.

William H. Taylor was born in Davidson County, Tenn., January 9, 1836, the son of Bartley and Mary Taylor. The father was born in Williamson County December 25, 1808. The parents came to Jones Creek, Dickson County, in 1861, where they are still living, making their home with William H. In the year 1861 our subject entered in the civil war, joining Company B, Forty-ninth Tennessee Regiment. He entered as orderly sergeant and was promoted to second lieutenant, which office he held till the close of the war. While at Atlanta, Ga., he received a severe wound in the right arm, disabling him for three months. In 1868 he was married to Mary E. Richardson. To them were born six children: Sallie W., Mary L., Henry T., Lavienia, Ellen J. and Edward. In his political views Mr. Taylor is a Democrat, and is a man of good standing among his fellow-citizens.

James J. Thompson was born July 13, 1842. His parents were Jeremiah and Angeline Thompson. The father was born December 7, 1801, and died March 2, 1864; the mother was born July 3,

1804, and died November 9, 1869. At the age of twenty our subject entered the Confederate Army as orderly sergeant, in 1862, joining Company E, Tenth Tennessee Cavalry, and served in the army until the surrender, when he returned home. He engaged in farming, which occupation he still follows. October 11, 1870, he was married to Irena S. Winstead. She was born in Humphreys County, Tenn., January 26, 1852. This union has resulted in seven children: Lela A., born September 11, 1871, and died March 18, 1873; Laura A., born January 30, 1873, and died January 21, 1874; Dorsey O., born August 7, 1875; Willie A., born September 30, 1877, died October 18, 1882; Heater L., born February 9, 1880; Lizzie M., born February 2, 1882, and Walter S., born May 5, 1884. Our subject and wife are members of the Methodist Episcopal Church South. Mr. Thompson is a Democrat.

Franklin Fulton Tidwell was born in Dickson County, Tenn., July 26, 1840, and was the eldest of nine children born to Moses and Nancy (McCaslin) Tidwell. Our subject was reared on a farm in his native county, living with his parents until the breaking out of the great civil war in 1861, when he enlisted in the Confederate Army, joining Company K, Eleventh Tennessee, of which company he was chosen first lieutenant, and afterward promoted to the captaincy. He was mustered into the service at Nashville, and served throughout the war. Returning to his native county he engaged in teaching school on Jones' Creek, near the present site of the town of Dickson. He then engaged in merchandising in Dickson, and was married while thus engaged, March 1, 1866, to Magdaline K. Petty, who was born in Hickman County, Tenn., January 8, 1848. This union has been blessed with ten children, all of whom are living: Mary Magdaline, born February 22, 1867; Nancy Hattie, born March 25, 1868; Hickman Benton, born August 23,1869; Susan Razelia, born August 14, 1871; Albert Sidney, born

February 24, 1873; Oscar Cromwell, bora August 28, 1874; Roberta Josephine, born February 14, 1876; Vina Kansas, born August 9, 1877; Anna Elizabeth, born June 24x 1881, and Frankie Pellham, born January 3, 1886. While the early educational advantages of our subject were limited he nevertheless acquired a good common school education and has kept well abreast of the times and current events. He is now engaged in farming, owning 500 acres of land situated one and a third miles south of Burns' Station. He is a Royal Arch Mason, being a member of Dickson Lodge, No. 478, F. & A. M., also a member of Charlotte Lodge, K. of H. He is an industrious and energetic man and is a stanch believer in the Democratic party. Hickman C., brother to our subject, was a brave and gallant soldier, going through the entire war and dying at the close at Greensboro, N. C.

Prof. W. T. Wade, proprietor and principal of Edgewood Normal School, Dickson County, Tenn., is a native of Lynchburg, Va., but is a graduate of the Lebanon Ohio College He plied his vocation in West Virginia, Missouri and Texas, and then came to Tennessee, taking charge of a school at Waverly, Humphreys County, for two years. In 1885 he leased the school property at Edgewood for twenty years, and established an excellent school where all the higher branches are taught. He possesses the highest confidence of the community and is particularly esteemed for the deep interest he takes in the educational and moral welfare of youth.

INDEX

www.ingramcontent.com/pod-product-compliance
Lightning Source LLC
LaVergne TN
LVHW051247080426
835513LV00016B/1789